Seen and Not Heard

*Memories of Childhood in the
Early 20th Century*

SEEN AND NOT HEARD

*Memories of Childhood in the
Early 20th Century*

G.K. NELSON

ALAN SUTTON

First published in the United Kingdom in 1993
Alan Sutton Publishing Ltd
Phoenix Mill · Far Thrupp · Stroud · Gloucestershire

First published in the United States of America in 1993
Alan Sutton Publishing Inc.
83 Washington Street · Dover · NH 03820

British Library Cataloguing in Publication Data

Nelson, Geoffrey K. (Geoffrey Kenneth) *1923-*
Seen and Not Heard : Memories of Childhood
in the Early 20th Century
I. Title
941.082092

ISBN 0-7509-0460-7

Library of Congress Cataloging in Publication Data
applied for

Cover illustration: At the Ashwell Spring, Longborough
(photograph courtesy of the Cotswold Countryside Collection, Northleach)

Typeset in 11/13 Bembo.
Typesetting and origination by
Alan Sutton Publishing Limited.
Printed in Great Britain by
The Bath Press, Avon.

CONTENTS

ACKNOWLEDGEMENTS

I am pleased to acknowledge the help I have received from over four hundred people in collecting the material for this book. In particular I am grateful to all those who have allowed me to publish edited versions of the material they have supplied and whose names are mentioned in the text. While many of the photographs have been sent in by those responding to my appeal, some have been purchased and others come from the postcard collections of my mother and mother-in-law. In some cases I have been unable to contact either the photographer or the original publisher of the photograph. However, if they will contact me I shall be pleased to correct this omission in any future edition.

I am grateful to Mrs Mary Sparks for her assistance in the collection of information, to Mrs Sylvia Kemp and Mr Ernest Kemp for their help with the transcription and typing of material and to my wife for advice and proof-reading.

G.K. Nelson
Northfield,
Birmingham

May 1993

INTRODUCTION

The phrase 'Children should be seen and not heard' from which the title of this book is derived seems to have originated in the Victorian period, although it was used until well into the twentieth century. Here those children who were seen and not heard have a chance to speak out about their early lives. Until the early part of the present century the majority of people remained illiterate meaning that few firsthand accounts exist of the lives of these ordinary people from earlier periods.

It is an aim of this project to record the memories of those whom the poet Thomas Gray described in his 'Elegy in a Country Churchyard' where he said

> Let not ambition mock their useful toil
> Their homely joys and destiny obscure,
> Nor Grandeur hear with a disdainful smile
> The short and simple annals of the poor.

The changing conditions of life during the first forty years of this century have made it difficult to define childhood. We have decided to define it as the period between birth and the age at which the young person is able to become independent of his/her parents or guardians. In the early part of the century this was legally defined to be twenty-one, but was later reduced to eighteen. However, the situation was always complicated by the fact that one could marry, with parents' consent, at the age of sixteen.

Some would argue that, because of the importance of economic independence, adulthood is arrived at when the young person starts work, or more realistically when his earnings enable him to be financially independent. Such definitions are sufficiently vague to cover wide periods of time and differences that are related to social class. For example, my grandfather started work when he was six, but would not have been financially independent until many years later, probably not much before he married at the age of nineteen. In earlier periods childhood merged gradually into adulthood, though most young persons would not be paid a full adult wage before the age of twenty-one.

Since the Second World War the term 'teenager' has been introduced and those over the age of twelve, to whom it might apply, are now offended if described as children, though in economic terms they remain schoolchildren until at least sixteen. Concerned as we are with the early years of this century, the term 'childhood' may be considered to cover persons up to the age of sixteen. This means that while most of our respondents left school at thirteen or fourteen we give some account of their experience of their first jobs and how they adapted to a working life.

In some ways young persons in their late teens in the 1930s and '40s were more mature than the teenagers of today, for while they received a shorter period of education they had been actively employed in commerce, industry or agriculture for a number of years, and had faced responsibilities that are now not met by many until they are well into their twenties. Attitudes to life and work today are very different from those that were dominant in the early years of the century and in this book we find expressions of the attitudes of those who were brought up in a world that has disappeared.

In conducting this study I have undertaken a project in historical anthropology. In recording and interpreting the memories of those who lived in a particular socio-cultural world that is as distant from the present as our society is from contemporary rural societies in India or Latin America, I have collected firsthand accounts of childhood from people living in many parts of England and Wales in the early part of the twentieth century and I hope that these will illustrate the quality of life during that period. Most relate to

country life but I have included one story of childhood in the city
to illustrate the differences between country and town.

In general my respondents' stories are told in their own words, as
given to me either in handwritten documents or recorded on tape
but some editing has been necessary. The work is illustrated with
photographs most of which have been supplied by respondents, and
postcards that illustrate contemporary attitudes towards children at
that time.

CHAPTER ONE

COTSWOLD DAYS

We start our exploration of childhood in England in the 1920s with this account from Mr Fred Townsend who was born and brought up in the Cotswolds.

My name is Fred Townsend and I was born in Oxfordshire, in a little town called Bampton on 19 December 1916. My father was a farm carter but he joined the Army and he was killed in action in France in 1916, three months before I was born. That left my mother as a young widow with me as a baby and she left Bampton and went to live with her sister who had two small children and had also been left a widow. We lived together at a place out in the Cotswolds called Kilkenny. My old grandfather worked on the farm there and I suppose he kept us and looked after us during the war.

In about 1920 my mother and her sister both married again and my stepfather took us to live at another little village in the Cotswolds. Before he went in the Army he had been a shepherd; he came from a long line of shepherds. We went out to live in this little village which was on the borders of Oxfordshire and Gloucestershire. It was a small village with about seventy or eighty cottages, down in the Windrush Valley. It had a village shop and a school and a church and there were four farms. All the men and boys who left school in the village worked on one or other of these four farms. All these farms had orchards, big orchards because every year in the autumn the cider grinders used to come round. They had a machine which they set up in the middle of the village and the farmers would bring all the apples they had picked in wagons and they would be tipped into one end of the machine and crushed and then it would come out as cider at the other end. I remember us children when we were on the way to school in those days, we used to take an old cup or something and catch a drop of the cider coming out one end and drink it.

The village school had two mistresses who had each got about twenty-five to thirty children to teach; there was about fifty to sixty children in the village going to school. There was the headmistress and the undermistress and they kept us in order. I don't know what teachers today do with that amount of children to look after, but those two old ladies kept us in order. One of them kept a cane hanging on the side of the cupboard and if you didn't behave yourself you got a whack with it.

Then, of course, there was the village shop; you could get practically anything there. It was a little general store kept by an old lady and her husband. All the children in the village went to the Church Sunday school and I remember that on Good Fridays we used to all be allowed to go into the wood. This was a big wood about 2 miles from the village. It was a private wood nobody could go into normally, but on Good Fridays we children were all taken. We used to walk up there and we had to pick primroses and take them back to the village and then on the Saturday the ladies would decorate the church with them ready for Easter Sunday. On Easter Sunday the vicar (he lived at the vicarage – there was a big vicarage in the village in those days) would give us hard-boiled painted eggs. I also remember on Whit Sunday the churchwarden, the clerk, would take all us children up on to the tower of the church. We went up this little winding dark stairway, some of us were a little bit frightened, but we used to come out right on the top of the church and there we could stand for a few minutes and look all over the village. That was a treat for us.

Of course we played all sorts of games. There was a hoop season, the boys would have a steel hoop and run with it, guiding it along with what we called a 'steel', a metal hook, and if you went down a hill, of course you could hold it back with the steel as well. Some of the girls used to knock along a wooden hoop with a stick but mostly the girls played skipping games and hopscotch and things like that. Us boys, of course, we played cricket and football and that in the streets. It was difficult, though, because the ball would go on to someone's garden and it was a job to get it back. Sometimes you could go to people and ask and they would let you have it but sometimes we had to just nip in and hope for the best that they didn't see us. Another big pastime with the boys was what we called 'fag cards'. In those days, you see, Players and Wills Woodbines in particular used to do series of cigarette cards. We used to beg them from the young chaps in the village. I can remember once I had a whole series of fifty cricketers, cards with people on them like Jack Hobbs and Sutcliffe, Larwood and Don Bradman, and Ponsford of Australia. I think a complete set in these days would be worth quite a bit of money but of course they have all gone now. What we used to do was to stick a card up on one end by the wall and then get back and flick cards at it and if you knocked that one down you had all the ones that were laying round about. If your card fell on to another one and covered it you could claim that card and the other one back, so in that way we could win or lose cards. Of course it was a matter of luck; sometimes you won and sometimes you lost.

Of course in the winter when it was a bit dusky we used to play all manner of games – running about, hide and seek and things like that. I am afraid we were a bit mischievous as well. We used to knock at people's doors and tap at the window and run away. I remember there was one poor old chap, he lived up a very narrow alley in a little house. His path ran straight from the door down to the gate. We used to go up there and lift the gate off the hinges, prop it up and whack a stone at the door and then run away down the alley. He would come running out after us and of course he went to push the gate open and he fell over on top of it, so that gave us a good chance to get away. I have often wondered now I am older, what a silly thing it was to do because the poor old man could easily have broken his legs but he never seemed to. We used to hear him come hollering down the road after us but he never caught us.

In those days all the people lived in little farm cottages – all the village houses were farm cottages at that time. Some of them were thatched, rather draughty and cold, and there was no central heating! We had just a coal fire or wood we picked up under the trees in the village. There was, of course, no electric light either. All the lighting we had was paraffin lamps or candles, and we used to take a candle up to bed. Mother used to always say, 'Be sure you blow the candle out, we don't want any fires', and of course she usually came up to see we were in bed and tucked in. In the winter when it was very cold I can remember she used to put a brick in the oven and hot it up and then wrap it up in some cloth and put it in the bed so it could warm the bed and we could warm our feet on it.

Of course there were no bathrooms in the houses, not even hot or cold water. We had to carry the water from the village pump. There were one or two pumps about in the village, and the women would go and carry a drop of water for drinking or washing or that. Sometimes even us children would go and fetch a drop, but in the evening the men used to go and they used to carry a couple of buckets of water, especially on Sunday nights. They would carry a lot of water to fill up the coppers for the women to do the washing, because washing day was, of course, on Mondays. They would fill up the old coppers in the wash-house, light the fire and the women would do all the washing on Monday mornings.

All the men in the village, of course, had a good garden and an allotment. They used to grow all their own vegetables, we always had plenty of potatoes and vegetables to eat. We used to eat a lot of bread and we had a bit of dripping or marge on that. I remember the baker used to come round once or twice a week. On a Saturday my mother used to buy a cake, so we had a bit of cake for tea on

Saturdays and Sundays. That was the only time, of course, that we had any cake. All the men usually kept a few chickens to get some eggs. Most of the cottagers kept a pig and that was fed on a bit of toppings from the miller and all the odd scraps that you had in the house. In the autumn you had the pig-killing time. They would kill the pig in the evening and then light a fire and put it on to burn all the bristles off. Then the butcher would clean it all down, wash it, scrub it and cut it up. The men used to share out the joints of meat. There were no fridges or deep freezers to keep it in, so they would share the meat out with the neighbours but the sides of bacon and hams would be salted in brine. Then, when they were dried out, they would be hung up so that through the winter you had some bacon and ham to cut at and use. About a week or a fortnight later somebody else would kill a pig and they would do the same – they would share the meat out, so through the winter time we usually had plenty of pork meat. The women would make all sorts of things as well; we had liver and fat and scratchings and things like that.

One of the problems in those old houses though was that you got a lot of mice in them. I can remember Dad setting mousetraps and catching mice. Then, of course, the farms had a lot of rats in those days. When the threshing machines came round to thresh the ricks of corn, us boys used to go down with sticks to kill the rats as they ran out of the ricks. It meant that if you had some poultry or pigsties you had rats about all round the village. It was the usual thing to go down the garden and see a rat running about. Of course, people kept cats and dogs and that helped keep them down a bit. I think during the Second World War the Ministry of Agriculture took that in hand and they poisoned a lot of them. There is nothing like the amount around these days. Of course, there were no indoor lavatories, only the old privies down the bottom of the garden and I remember if we had to go down there at night in the dark, we used to kick the door and make a good old noise and rattle on the door in case there was a rat in there.

Another thing in those villages, out in the Cotswolds, we used to have the fox and hounds about and when the hounds were about we used to run to see them and watch them. Down in the Windrush Valley, at the river, the otter hunters used to come as well. They used to walk along the banks of the river and let the dogs go into the river and flush out the otters. Us children in the holidays used to walk along the banks and follow them. There was a little stream in the village in which we used to catch minnows and chubbies in jam jars and take them home but, of course, they didn't last very long. I can remember as children too we used to have to take our fathers' tea up into the hay fields and the harvest fields. We used to take the tea up after school and sit and have our tea up in the field with our dads.

As far as I can remember there were only two motor cars in the village and then the vicar bought a car, which made three. The old vicar used to go to some of the villages round about to do visiting. If he went out in his car he used to always take a few of us boys with him. We thought it was good to go and have a ride but usually something went wrong with his car and he didn't know anything about it and that meant that we had to get out and push him back home. That was his way of getting back – just take some of us boys to push him back to the village.

When I was about eleven years old my stepfather moved from that farm to another one. It was 2 miles outside a little town, quite lonely. We had to walk the 2 miles to school. There was a schoolmaster, he was a right old tartar too, he used to whack it into us if we didn't behave. I had always had a lot of bronchial trouble and when I was thirteen I had an illness, I think it was double pneumonia. I was very ill for a long time and the doctor said I would have to be very careful and I never went back to school. In fact I left school at that age, thirteen. I used to have to lay down a lot in the summer. It was a good summer that year and I used to lay on a mattress outside the house, sometimes in the garden. There was a lady who lived nearby. She was very kind and used to bring me a lot of books and magazines and I did a lot of reading that year and I think I probably educated myself more than if I had been at school. I found that a great help to me in later years.

I remember Saturday evenings were bath nights and at that time we used to bath in front of the fire in a big tin bath. Mother would heat the water in the copper and then we would go in the bath when we were little, one after the other. When the water began to get cold she would scoop some out in a bucket and put another bucket of hot in. The first child would go in and then get out and dry himself and then the next would go in. We were bathed, boys and girls, all one after the other. We never took any notice of one another when we were small. Of course, when we got a bit older us boys had to bath out in the wash-house. The girls still bathed in front of the kitchen fire but us boys had to keep out of the way then, or else we had to go to bed earlier while they had their bath. We didn't think a lot of that but that was how things had to be done. You see, those farm cottages only had two bedrooms usually and Dad and Mother would be in one with, perhaps, the youngest child and us others, boys and girls, had to sleep all in the same room. Sometimes there were one or two in a bed and some of the families in the village were much bigger than ours and I don't know how they managed – two or three boys in one bed and two or three girls in the other.

There were one or two other things about my childhood too, you know. I can remember seeing my first aeroplane. It went over and we were allowed to go out in the school yard to see it go across and that was a big thrill in those days. I can also remember being told about the birth of the little Princess Elizabeth, our present Queen. That was a big thing. In the winter evenings we used to sit round the table and play games like ludo, dominoes and things like that and our parents used to play games with us. We had more of a fellowship, we lived more as a family. There was no television in those days and, in fact, the wireless was only just coming in and they were very few and far between. You had to have headphones to listen in to them and not many people in the village had got them. I remember being taken in to a friend's house, and they put the headphones on and let me listen to some music. They told me it was coming from London and we thought it was a marvellous thing.

When I got to fourteen, I had recovered a bit from my illness and like all the children I had to find a job and go to work. In those days all the boys went to work on the farm, you see, and the girls went to work in the big houses, in service. The first place I went to work on was a little dairy farm and we used to deliver milk round the little town, morning and afternoon. I worked there for two years and we used to deliver twice a day, seven days a week, Sundays, Bank Holidays and all. In that two years I only had one Sunday afternoon off. He was a very good farmer and he was very good to me. He paid me 6s a week (30p in present day money) and if there was plenty of milk about he used to give me a pint of milk to take home to Mother. With this 6s I used to give 5s to Mother and she gave me 1s back. I had to save 6d of that towards buying clothes and the other 6d. I used to spend. I can remember buying a 2d magazine, the *Magnet*. When I was a bit older I used to have a film magazine instead of the *Magnet*.

When I worked on this little dairy farm the first job in the morning was to carry the milk from the milking shed up to the dairy, where the farmer's wife would put it through the cooler and bottle it ready for delivery. There was a row of houses up by this farm and I used to have a little truck and load it up with crates of milk and push it up the lane and deliver to these houses. When I got back the milking had all been finished and they were loading up ready to go round the town. The farmer had a motor bike with a specially equipped side-car; it was like a long, oblong, great wooden box thing and we used to load the crates of milk into it, then off we went round the town. The farmer used to deliver down one side of the road and I went down the other. When we got back later in the morning I used to have to wash the bottles and wash and clean up the dairy ready for when we did it all again in the afternoon.

I used to make up by doing odd jobs until milking time in the afternoon. I used to make butter, I remember, in a little churn. The farmer's wife put the cream into this little churn and you had to wind the handle round till the butter formed. It was only a little churn but sometimes it took well over an hour to make the butter. The farmer's wife was very pleased when it was made and so was I because turning this handle was really hard work. You had to keep going and not stop, you see, or else the butter wouldn't make. Then I used to do other jobs on the farm till it was time to fetch the cows. That was my job about 2 o'clock, to fetch the cows in ready for milking again. I used to take the old dog with me and he used to round them up if they were scattered about. Sometimes the old bull would be out in the field and I can remember that on one occasion he came for me. He was a bit nasty that day and he came for me and I took to my heels. I just dived under the fence as he ploughed up the ground behind me with his horns, so I was lucky to get away that day.

They had an old horse and a little trap and I used to drive that round the farm and do little odd jobs. I remember the first day the old farmer told me to go and harness the horse – I had never done that before. To put a horse's collar on you have to put it on upside down, with the wider end put over his head, and then twist it round. I didn't know this and I was trying to push it on the poor old horse's head with the narrow side up. I couldn't get it on and I had to go and tell the farmer and he had to come and do it.

The farmer was very good to me but sometimes, when we got back from the afternoon delivery at 5 o'clock he would ask me to stop and wash the bottles at night because him and his wife wanted to go out. If that happened he used to give me 6d extra or else perhaps one night he would take me with them to the cinema, and he would pay for me to go in. That was a real good treat for me. I can remember on one or two occasions he took me to Stow Fair, a big horse fair. The gypsies used to come and bring all sorts of horses and sell them to the farmers and you would see the various farmers, when they wanted a horse, they would go there and pick one out. Of course, you had to be careful because some of the horses had something the matter with them. We heard a story at one time, I don't know whether it was true or not, about an old farmer who bought a horse and apparently it had been in a circus. One day they were working it and one of the young chaps started playing a mouth organ and the horse stood up on its hind legs and started dancing. I don't know whether that was right but I should think the old farmer was a bit concerned.

I worked on the farm for those two years and at that time, when a boy got to sixteen, the farmer had to start paying insurance for him and this farmer, he didn't reckon to do that. Once a boy got to sixteen he had to leave and the farmer would get another younger boy out of school to work there for another two years. I was very sorry to leave, but, as I say, he was a good man, he was very good to me and I enjoyed working there. When the time came then, I had to go and work on the bigger farm where my stepfather worked and, of course, once I got on this bigger farm I began the harder farm work, including ploughing, manure carting and spreading, and harvesting, as it was in those days.

CHAPTER TWO

A NORFOLK CHOIR BOY

Mr Edward Sherwood was born in Downham Market, Norfolk, but left to find work in Brighton in 1926. He was living in Worthing when he contacted me in 1988 with the information reported here. I have subsequently attempted to contact him without success. He opens his account by remarking:

Being Norfolk born and bred we tend to stay that way. My early days are very clear in my mind.

I was born at the lower end of a lane called Ryston End (at Downham Market). It is still there, although the house has been altered and is now a solicitor's office. I was born at 6 p.m. on 7 April 1908 and my mother was assisted by the local midwife, the birth taking place in the family four-poster bed. At that time my father was a foreman of blacksmiths at an agricultural engineering company on the London Road.

The house was rent free, on the understanding that my father made up the weekly time-sheets. This house had four bedrooms and three large rooms below. An old grandfather clock stood in the corner of the living-room. A hole was cut into the floor to stand the clock in to allow for it being taller than the room's height. Next door was another house and next to that was the local police court. Beyond that was the drive to the workhouse. On court days we often had some excitement. Many of the crimes were offences like riding a bicycle without lights or poaching. The fine for riding without lights was generally 5s. Poaching was more serious if there had been a previous offence, and a sentence of six or twelve months could be given.

My father and his two boys by his first marriage all worked at the works opposite. My mother slaved at home – no running water and no bathroom. We had a pump in a small yard at the back. Washing day was purgatory for us all. Lighting was by paraffin lamps or candles.

We had one exciting day when a builder's paint store caught fire. Our fire engine, which was hand-pumped with four men each side and which had been bought from Baker Street, London, proved to be useless, so the place burnt out. In those days we could spin our tops on the A10 which was the main road.

In due course I was sent to school, aged four years. I was taken by my brother, aged five-and-a-half, and handed over to Mrs Brown, afterwards a lifelong friend. We had proper lessons, full time. I walked to and from school, including during lunch hour as there were no school meals. Children who lived further away brought sandwiches, which were mainly bread and jam. They ate them round the fires in the classrooms, but in the summer they stayed in the playground. They drank water; there was only one iron cup between 165 children and we all caught every childish complaint that was going.

The lessons in what was known as the 'babies' class' included writing on slates or sand trays with wooden skewers. In the higher classes we were taught 'copperplate' style handwriting. Even in those early days we were caned or smacked, usually on the wrist.

In due course we went in to the Boys' School, which was at the other end of the school block. That was when I was eight in 1916, when the war had been on for two years. During that time we had many changes of teacher, ladies replacing men. We were punished for very little and quite often, but we became toughened to it.

In those days we were seated on forms, five children in a row. I was left-handed and a nuisance, so I was made to use my right hand. I stammered badly up to the age of twenty and had to take a lot of mocking from both school fellows and my own brothers. I had a miserable time for years. I couldn't recite and still can't. I found singing in the church choir a help and I taught myself breathing exercises. It is only since the Second World War that I have been able to control it completely. That teacher from Denver has much to answer for!

My brothers were called up during the First World War and they would have taken Father too but he was very deaf, due to his work. Just before the outbreak of war my father had started his own business. His sons, my stepbrothers, were to do the shoeing and general smithy work, while he did reaper binders and other farm machinery. He was well known among farmers over a wide area and always had plenty of work, but the sons were called up and my brother and I were called on to work after school. My brother did not like it much so he wriggled out when he could. I was not artful enough so I got caught for turning the drilling machine, blowing the fire, working in awkward places and my pet aversion – turning the grind stone. It was a new one, about 5 ft in diameter. I had to stand on a box to reach it.

At the end of the war my two stepbrothers came home from the war but they were very unsettled. The elder went over to making motor bikes from ex-WD parts. The youngest just disappeared and I have never seen him since. That left father on his own, and then he fell ill. The eldest brother took over the shop for his motor bikes. Father died in 1923 after a long illness, leaving us in poor circumstances. Doctors had to be paid in those times.

My own brother and two sisters were left with mother. My brother went to work for a baker and I went as errand boy to a draper. When my older sister left school she went to be a maid and the younger sister became a dressmaker's apprentice. When I left school I went to work full time at the shop where I had been errand boy and earned 10s a week. My brother earned more than that. All we had to live on was his money and mine plus what my mother could earn by taking in washing, laying out dead people or sitting with sick people.

We had little recreation. I had my first holiday when I was fourteen, we went to Snettisham. I made a tent from old shop blinds which I begged from my employer. I made jointed poles from bamboo. We hired bicycles for 2*d* a day and we biked to Snettisham beach, taking some food with us. For a week we made our camp and played in the sea and on the beach. Then the wind got up and so did our tent. I did not realize that the blind had been replaced because it was rotten. So we dumped it and came home a day early. We would have liked to have joined the Scouts but there wasn't a troop in Downham. In any case we could not have afforded the outfit, about 30*s*.

In due course I had rises in pay – to 16*s* by the time I was sixteen. Then an uncle of mine who had a shop in Wimbotsham asked me to work for him for 20*s*, which I did, having to walk there and back, a distance of 1½ miles. I started work at 8 a.m. finishing at 6 p.m.

On Saturdays in company with another lad we went round the nearby fens with an old coach and horse delivering groceries etc. to outlying houses. We started at 8 a.m. and got back about 9 p.m. Then we had to cash up and turn the horse out to grass, getting home about 10 p.m. Working as we had to in those times, we had all the exercise we needed.

I started Sunday school at the age of three, being taken by my brother, then aged four-and-a-half. Living as we did in Downham Market, which in those days was a very quiet place as cars were almost non-existent and there were only a few horses in use on Sundays, there was very little danger on the roads.

After Sunday school we then walked up to the church for the remainder of the morning service. The church was reasonably full – the children were in the north aisle, the centre was occupied by the local tradesmen and their wives, local farmers, doctors and the rest of the 'élite'. The balcony was used by some of the more 'toffee-nosed'.

At the age of eight I joined the choir. There were about twenty boys, eight men and a few ladies, mainly singing alto. Also behind the organ were the seats where the girls from Miss Markham's School sat. This was not a good idea as they faced the choir boys. You can imagine the giggles, and dirty looks from the teachers.

In the south aisle, as near the door as possible, were seated the paupers all dressed in very patched and mended grey. They were put near the door so they could leave quickly without having to rub shoulders with the élite.

The services followed a regular pattern. Holy Communion once a month except for special dates, Easter, Whitsun, Christmas and so on. On Good Friday we had a three hour service and Litany once a month.

The choir was paid 25*s* per year with a reduction of 1*d* for not coming to practice and 2*d* for missing a service. Payment was quarterly.

While I was there we had a musical festival in Ely Cathedral. There were choirs from all over the diocese. It was an occasion I have never forgotten and it made a deep impression on me. You must remember that the church organ and choir was the only time most of us ever heard any music.

However, in due course my voice broke (when I was thirteen) and I left the choir and with the arrival of motor bikes in my family, my father and elder brother having them, the church became rather neglected.

During this time the local nonconformists were quite numerous in Downham. We had four Wesleyan chapels and a Baptist church. These were well attended and usually the church evening service was over first. We could hear the closing hymn in the nearby chapel. We boys were always struck by the liveliness and vigour of the hymns.

In those days the church and chapels seldom mixed. We had a manse three doors from where we lived and I never spoke to the minister. Our Sunday school treats, usually taken at Hunstanton, were never on the same day and I can't remember there ever being an exchange of pulpits.

CHAPTER THREE

A
DERBYSHIRE
CHILDHOOD

Mrs Spencer evokes the atmosphere of life in a village in the Peak District.
Her frank description of her grandparents takes us into the heart of family
life at that time.

My childhood in the tiny village of Great Hucklow in the late
1920s and up to the last war was an extremely happy one, in spite
of the fact that we were definitely among the 'have-nots'. But,
perhaps with only a small handful of exceptions, we were in tune
with the rest of the villagers. We had to 'scrat and scrape' to make
ends meet but as my dad used to say 'we owed nowt'. We were rich
in love from our parents and grandparents, a commodity which
seems sadly lacking today.

Village community life had changed very little from the end of
the nineteenth century to the 1930s The older female inhabitants
still wore long skirts down to the ground. Everyone had a Sunday
chapel outfit. For the men, mostly farmers, it was almost a uniform,
black suit, white shirt, celluloid collar, black tie, hard hat and heavy
duty highly polished black boots. I can still hear Herbert Hoyle
squeaking down the chapel aisles doing the collection after the
sermon. The collection wasn't put on a plate for all to see. It was
deposited, ever so discreetly, in a box with a 'mouth'. Often my

brother and I were told that all my mother had in the house was 6*d*, saved for the collection. She and Dad each put in 2*d*, Frank and I a penny each. The biblical story of the widow's mite had real meaning for us! There was no more money then until Dad brought home his wages the following weekend, unless someone wanted eggs. We had a poultry farm on the hillside. The price of eggs varied from 9*d* to 1*s* 3*d* a dozen, according to whether the hens were in good lay.

My mother had served her apprenticeship in dressmaking and tailoring after leaving school. My brother and I had all our clothes home-made, often from something bought at a jumble sale, unpicked, washed and re-cut. My mother was a wizard. I had my first bought coat, a harris tweed, at the age of twenty-one when I went to college. Sometimes she did sewing and alterations for people, but they never wanted to pay much. My father worked on the railway, although he hadn't always done so. He and his twin brother had worked on a farm for several years until just before the First World War. My father then went to Bolsover, where he lodged with a miner's family working for the LMS Railway. His brother joined the Manchester Regiment on the outbreak of war and was killed on the Somme.

My paternal grandfather Townsend came from a tiny hamlet over the moors called Abney. He was a real character and my brother and I were scared stiff of him. He was a drystone waller. Some of his work is still standing unblemished today. I noticed it when I visited the village in 1984. The trouble was, that work was sporadic and Grandad liked his pint. He married my grandmother in the early 1890s. They had a pokey two-up, two-down cottage in the Back Fold, a lane in the village. During the summer I believe they scratched along, but the winters were hard. I remember my dad telling us how he hated being sent with an empty bucket, knocking on doors begging coal. When it was returned it was usually a bucket of slack, with a few lumps on the top for disguise.

Granny Townsend was a tattle-box and loved to make mischief. She also loved to lie in bed. I suppose she was feckless, but with a husband who 'drank' his wages on the way home, who could blame her. It was this very feckless way of life which caused the death of one of her daughters. The children were all downstairs on their own, when the little girl's night-dress caught fire. She died later in hospital from these burns. The shock of seeing his little sister so badly burned had such a profound effect on my father that he feared fire for the rest of his life. He even begged that after death, we wouldn't have his body cremated.

The death of his daughter also had a profound effect on my grandad. He turned 'religious' and stopped drinking. One of my earliest recollections is of him coming up the lane with one fist stuck high above his head as he constantly prayed aloud for forgiveness. This went on from 1902 when Aunt Lucy was burned, until the day he died at the roadside in 1937. He was walking to Tideswell to collect his pension one frosty morning. Climbing the last hill his heart stopped. My father, going to work on his motor bike, was the one who found him. He was eighty-six years of age.

Whenever there was a sale in the locality Grandad used to go and buy a bucket of books for 6d. He had dozens of books, mostly in faded marble covers. Most of them were history, ancient history about the Greeks and Romans. He read every one. As no-one had electricity in their homes it was literally oil lamps and candles. My grandad used to lie down on the settle and stick a candle on his chest with hot wax. Then he put his specs on the end of his nose and held his book beyond the candle. Often he would fall asleep and Granny would blow out the candle. Frequently, during the summer, he used to call at our bungalow on the way to the woods. He would announce that he was going for a stick and wanted to borrow our saw. Grandad's stick was usually a tree trunk about 10 to 15 ft long with the branches trimmed off. He used to hoist it on one shoulder, stick his loose fist in the air and march off home praying. Sometimes a gang of us children would march behind him, imitating him. Usually he ignored us but occasionally he would turn round and 'look'. We all fled.

You never saw Grandad without his old pipe stuck in the corner of his mouth. As children, my brother and I often wondered whether he took it out when in bed. We never dared to ask. Sometime in the early thirties he began to complain of a sore on his lip, in the corner of his mouth just where his pipe always rested. None of the usual remedies did any good, so eventually the local GP sent him to see a specialist in Sheffield. Cancer was diagnosed. Grandad was one of the first patients to be treated with Radium needles. The cancer was burnt away leaving a deep hollow in the corner of his mouth where it had been. But he still continued to smoke his old pipe, drooping at an odd angle down to his chin.

My grandmother Townsend, too, was quite a character. She did her best to make mischief between my parents. I can still recall lying in bed on Friday nights, listening to them both going 'at it' hammer and tongs after Dad had paid his mother her weekly visit. After I was born, my mother was very ill through neglect at my birth. Granny always said she was 'putting it on'. Her boast was that she didn't know what a headache was – after having six children, including two sets of twins. Just after her eightieth birthday she developed a pain in her chest. So she went to bed and stopped there, complaining that she 'felt badly'. The doctor told her it was indigestion, to take some 'bi-carb', get up and walk about. She wouldn't. With lying in bed and being a large woman anyway, she developed dropsy. The doctor came every day and tried to get her up and doing but she wouldn't budge. In a fortnight she was dead. I can remember the doctor coming to our house and scratching his head, saying he couldn't put 'indigestion' on her death certificate, as no-one would believe him.

My maternal grandparents, in contrast, were quite widely travelled. Grandad Hayto was a heating engineer and worked for a firm called Brightsides of Sheffield. He was sent all over the country fulfilling contracts and the family usually went with him. They all lived in London for a time, while he was installing central heating in the old War Office. Another time he was in Stornaway putting central heating in the castle. I think they finally settled in Great Hucklow after Grandad left Brightsides and set up in business on his own. He and Granny had two children, my mother Mabel and, of course, her brother, Arthur. Then tragedy struck. Arthur had always been regarded as a dunce at school until a new headmaster quickly spotted he was profoundly deaf. He died of meningitis just about the time I was born in 1924. I used to practically live with my grandparents during the summers of my early childhood. Grandad had two motor bikes with side-cars. One was called Gussy, and the other Bessie. Gussy had an oblong box-like side-car designed for carrying lengths of pipe and tools. Grandad put central heating in most of the Peak District schools. A lot of this work was done during the summer holidays and I went with him, sitting most uncomfortably on a 'flock' cushion among the paraphernalia in the side-car. Then he suffered a stroke which left him very disabled and business more or less ground to a halt. I don't honestly know what my grandparents lived on after that, although I believe they had an old age pension, such as it was. Grandad finally died of another massive stroke in 1935. My brother and I were in constant awe of him because he wouldn't stand any nonsense. Even the cats jumped to his bidding. I can visualize him now, sitting in his squeaky creaky basket chair, with his legs up on another one and a cat sprawled down each leg. Grandad had only to reach for an old leather strap, call 'box' and the cats would vanish. So would we; Grandad wasn't averse to using that strap on us if he thought we deserved it.

In his younger days, when commuting between Hucklow and Sheffield, Grandad used to sometimes call at a pawnbroker's shop and buy something. I have still one or two of his 'treasures' which I intend to pass down to my children. One is a silver-plated teapot. I've tried to match it, to make a tea-set, many times but haven't had any luck. Another is a wall clock which has pride of place in my home. Mother also had a very good brass-faced barometer but I don't know where that went. I suspect it was sold for a song with their effects in 1972.

Granny Hayto was in service in Bakewell when she met and married Grandad. Her family came from the Belper area. My knowledge of Granny's background is rather sketchy but I believe her mother died when she was a child. Her dad married again and her stepmother couldn't wait to get rid of her. She was more or less brought up by her grandmother who was in service at Lea Hurst, the home of Florence Nightingale's mother. She married a footman and Mrs Nightingale gave them a tea service as a wedding present. It has always been handed down to the daughter of the family. So I have it.

Granny didn't live long after Grandad had died. I think she pined for him. We, that is Mum, Dad, my brother and myself, went to live with her after Grandad's death, renting the poultry farm and bungalow to some people. That was not very successful financially as they were always behind with the rent, so Mum and Dad sold the smallholding for a pittance. Granny finally died suddenly of a seizure in 1937 and was buried in the chapel yard with Grandad.

Funerals in the village were quite something. There was no such thing as cremation. The body was usually laid out in the sitting-room by a village woman, who was always called upon to do this service. Everyone came to view the body and pay their respects, children included, unless the dead person's face was not a pleasant sight. At the funeral the coffin was hoisted on the shoulders of the bearers and carried to the chapel, with the mourners walking behind. This was also the procedure in the two hamlets near to Great Hucklow − Windmill and Grindlow. The bearers had to carry the coffin a good half mile. After the service the mourners went back to the home of the deceased for a ham tea. That's when, in our family, the silver teapot was used. Everyone wore funeral black, spoke in hushed tones and crept around as silently as possible. From the moment of death until after the funeral, all the curtains were drawn in that house as well as in the houses en route to the chapel. I can remember how dark everywhere seemed to be. We children were not allowed to play our usual games and were expected to adopt long faces like everyone else. One funeral in the family comes to mind quite vividly because my brother and I got into terrible trouble afterwards. It was an uncle called Abram. He and Auntie Annie lived in a tiny one-up, one-down end cottage in the Back Fold. The bedroom was reached by a narrow winding chair. Uncle Abram was a big man and the bearers couldn't get the coffin down the stairs without tipping it on end. Unfortunately, they tipped the poor man head downwards and as the coffin was manoeuvred, from inside it came a long drawn out moan. My aunt squealed that he was still alive and my brother and I were seized with the giggles. I fear we were very irreverent children.

There were two chapels in the village, the Methodist chapel on the corner and the Unitarians down Dirty Lane – so called because it usually was, being pre-Tarmacadam. Our parish church was at Hope, 5 miles away across the fields and much further by road. Mum and Dad were married at Hope church in 1922. Once a month the vicar used to walk over the fields on a Sunday afternoon to conduct a short service in the school. The altar was enclosed in a big, long cupboard along one wall in a large classroom. As small children we used to look at it and wonder what it was! I think about half a dozen people attended the service, my mother being one.

The Methodist chapel was always busily involved in the community. In June there were the Sermons, for which the pews were packed to capacity. Staging was put up in tiers for the Sunday school children to sit on and we had to learn two special hymns to sing by ourselves. Forms and chairs were squashed in all round the pulpit for the choir. My mum and dad were in the Great Hucklow choirs and at least two anthems were sung. Our village choir was always augmented by choirs from Bradwell, Foolow and Little Hucklow. They came and sang at our Sermons and we sang at theirs. There was a lot of comings and goings at Sermons time. Visitors taking part in our Sermons had new clothes and it was regarded as a very socially exciting occasion.

The Sermons were followed by the Harvest Festival which ended with the produce being sold for chapel funds and a potato pie supper. The pies were made by our village housewives and there was usually competition to sit at the table where a certain housewife's pie would be served as it was noted for its lovely succulent filling and light pastry.

But for us children, the most exciting time was Christmas. The Sunday school was expected to produce a concert. I always had to learn a recitation and usually forgot my lines half-way through from sheer terror. Two poems chosen by my mother still come to mind – 'Has anyone seen my mouse?', when I had to stand on the wobbly stage, clutching an empty box, and the poem about Christopher Robin saying his prayers. The concert was well-padded out with various turns by talented villagers who sang, or played an instrument. My father used to recite poems in dialect. He was good too! On Christmas Eve the chapel choir went carol singing through three villages, Great Hucklow, Grindlow and Windmill. Older children were allowed to go and join in, but no young children. In fact, for children to go carol singing on their own was unheard of. The repertoire wasn't very large, about six old favourites, usually requested at the 'ports of call'. One favourite was 'Peace o'er the World'. The music was written by a local man many years previously. Until recently, I had the score of this carol as my mother was very musical and had studied harmony. She wrote it down. I've since searched for it but it seems to be mislaid. It was a great treat to be allowed to go with the choir as they had various traditional stopping places such as farms and 'big' houses, where refreshments wet and festive were waiting. It entailed a good 5 or 6 mile trudge round the three villages, but nobody minded!

Sometimes the Sunday school party was held between Christmas and the New Year. I used to hate it as it got very boisterous and silly kissing games were played. The Sunday school superintendent, Herbert Hoyle, was à nice, well meaning man but he couldn't control the older children, who took advantage of him. As far as I was concerned, the best party was the one held by the Unitarians at Barleycrofts, to which all the village schoolchildren were invited. This party was beautifully organized every year and to my brother and myself, it was one of our Christmas highlights.

The real magic of Christmas to us children was naturally the expectation of a visit from Santa Claus. Compared with today and what children are led to expect through the constant bombardment of advertising, our expectations were very low. We were never disappointed, however, and looking back I realize what a lot of scrimping and saving our parents had done to provide our small presents. One of Dad's socks was carefully hung at the bottom of the bed. In it was usually a bright new penny, stuffed into the toe, followed by a shiny apple and an orange. These were followed by little games and toys and finally topped off by a pink sugar pig. We always had an annual and a box of chocolate animals, teddy bears for Frank and mice for me. Mother used to make things for us to wear. One year I had a pair of fur backed gloves. Other presents I can recall from different Christmases were a china tea-set, a big celluloid doll I called Rosie, and a doll's push-chair. Frank had the equivalent in boy's things. He had a Hornby train set with a circular track one year and after that there was usually something added, like a signal-box, more trucks or lines. To my brother and me, these gifts were the ultimate. We never had money to spend like today's children but we never felt in any way deprived.

We both had to help on the poultry farm cleaning out the hen-houses, making sure the water pots were replenished and collecting eggs. For this, if funds were good, we each got a Saturday penny to spend on sweets. But more often than not it was a penny between us and sometimes even a halfpenny to share. Oh the thrill on Saturday morning of rushing headlong down the lane to Nellie Longden's shop and deciding what to buy. It had to be something that would last, such as humbugs or aniseed balls, and something which gave a lot for a penny. We used to look through the window before entering to see which of the two sisters was in the shop. If it was Nellie, we waited, because she weighed everything very, very carefully but if Annie was there, we would rush in quickly because Annie wasn't so fussy and we would get another sweet or two in the bag.

The minister of the Unitarian chapel was a Revd L. du Garde
Peach. He had been minister there since my father was a boy. My
father and the other village children grew up with his two sons.
One son, Arnold, was strange. He was never allowed out of the
house or the garden. I think he may have been epileptic and was
looked after by the cook/housekeeper named Ginny. The other son
became famous as a playwright. In fact, my parents can remember
Laurie Peach writing plays when a boy. He used to inveigle them to
take part and put on a show for which he charged two pins. The
Peach boys didn't attend the village school, but according to my
parents, you couldn't meet a nicer, kinder family anywhere. They
were greatly respected by everyone.

Laurie wrote many plays which were broadcast by the BBC. I
can well remember his 'Castles of England' series which came on
Children's Hour and were also published in book form. Perhaps it
was these plays that triggered off my interest in history. He could
always be relied upon to provide a play of local interest when the
occasion arose, often gently lampooning various local citizens who
always took it in good part. He used to organize concerts every
year in the Holiday Homes and after the interval there would be
one of his special one act plays. I can remember one in particular
which told the story of Derwent Village which was going to be
submerged in the new reservoir being built – Ladybower in the
Peak District. He also introduced the village to William
Shakespeare! He produced a Shakespeare play every winter – all the
actors taking part were local people, with no professional
experience as such, but the plays were of a very high standard and
were presented every night for a week. Needless to say, the room
was always packed to capacity. In the village was an old cupola
where in times gone by lead had been smelted. It had fallen into
disuse since all the local lead mines had been worked out. Laurie
Peach bought it and converted it into a theatre. It was magnificent.
From the outside nothing was changed but inside, although he left
the walls of rough limestone untouched, a stage was added and tiers

of seating which gave everyone an uninterrupted view. People came from London and Manchester to see his productions.

Easter used to herald the start of the summer visits of the 'holiday homers', as they were known to us. The homes were five or six wooden huts with galvanized iron roofs, built in a field at the edge of the village. They were owned and run by the Unitarian church. The holiday homers were bus-loads of children, brought every week for a country holiday. Mostly they were the 'have-nots' of Manchester and children from orphanages. I can remember their visits quite clearly although they never mixed with the village children. Occasionally there would be some friction and name-calling when we locals took our 'dandies' and floats to the troughs for drinking water. There was no piped drinking water in the village until the late 1930s so all the water had to be carried from the troughs. These were filled with water which came from somewhere out of the ground and was never known to dry up, even in times of drought. Being in a limestone area, the district was riddled with underground springs and wells. There was a well in our lower croft, with steps leading down into it and one in the school playground which was covered by an enormous slab. About ten years ago I met the headmaster of the school at a conference and he was telling me about a constant damp problem they had in a newly built classroom. When I told him there was a well under the floor he was amazed. Someone had not done their homework prior to that building programme.

A few weeks ago, I happened to glance through the kitchen window at High Ridge and saw, in the fields beyond our garden, a sight which truly horrified me. The grass in these two fields is allowed to grow for hay during the summer and there, in the knee high grass, was a man and his children romping with a dog. In my childhood years such behaviour was unheard of. Mowed grass was a precious commodity and anyone walking through these fields kept to the paths. We children knew this and never walked in long mowing grass. When harvest time arrived, it was very hard work and everyone, man, woman and child, buckled to and helped while the weather held. There was very little mechanization. It was hard human slog with hayrake and pitchfork. When the blisters on your hands broke and bled, you wrapped a rag round and kept going. When the field of hay was finally raked into 'cobs', we all breathed a sigh of relief and prayed for a nice day tomorrow. Every farmer had a cart and several horses and they all waded in to help each other. We children loved it, especially riding on top of a load of hay to the barn where our job was to tread the hay and make sure it was spread evenly. It's a miracle we weren't stabbed many times with all the pitchforks waving about. Sometimes the children's job was to take dinner out to the workers. Huge slabs of bread and cheese, cold pie and bottles of cold tea. Hay was the main crop in those days. Not much corn was grown or roots as the farms were all on the edge of the moors and I don't suppose the soil was very suitable. Pesticides were unheard of and as far as I can recall, manure was the only fertilizer ever spread during winter.

During the summer holidays from school there was the annual Sunday school trip by charabanc. Most children were accompanied by their parents, but as my father was always at work and Mother couldn't leave the poultry, my brother and I were put in the care of Mr Hoyle, the superintendent. I can't remember much about these trips except that, as often as not, it rained and we had colds afterwards. To most children this was the only holiday they were likely to get. We never went away for longer than a day as it meant a lot of planning to get someone to look after the poultry for us. Because he worked on the railway, our father had several free passes each year. These were used to take us on days out. I can remember several trips to London and also to Liverpool, where we went on the overhead railway to Seaforth sands, seeing many ships in dry dock on the way. Sadly that is all gone now.

Talking of Sunday school outings, Mum and Dad used to tell us about their outings as children. They went to Darley Dale in a 'brake', whatever that was, where the more adventurous caught a train at Darley Dale station and went to Matlock – all of 3 miles! Then they walked back. I can also remember my father telling us about the first motor cars passing near the village when he was a boy. They must have been very noisy because they were heard almost leaving Tideswell, 2½ miles away. The children would run down Dirty Lane in time to see the vehicle go past.

In the 1930s only one family in the village owned a car and that was because he owned a small cutlery business in Sheffield. There were seveal motor bikes, however, and everyone had a push-bike. You needed it. The public transport situation was virtually non-existent. Buses plied between Buxton and Sheffield. During the summer there was a bus each way every hour; in spring and autumn every two hours; and during the winter months every four hours. In bad weather there might not be a bus at all. The winter of 1933 was unusually severe. It snowed non-stop for nearly four days and nights. Our bungalow was almost buried and the bus was stuck in a drift at Windmill. The few passengers and the driver and the conductor were rescued by a farmer. All the villages were cut off and the village shop quickly ran out of the basic foods, so the men took sacks and walked over the fields to Tideswell. Normally, the roads were kept open by the farmers who used their horses to pull snow ploughs. These were long, heavy wooden structures. We children loved it, as we were allowed to sit on the plough to help to hold it down.

Until quite recently the letters EC were frequently included in the description of a house for sale in country areas. EC was an abbreviation of earth closet. In Great Hucklow, prior to water being piped to the village, all the houses had ECs or, like us, an 'Elsan' lavatory. WCs were unheard of! Where there was a row of small cottages, such as the Back Fold, one EC served them all! The EC was usually situated quite a distance from the house; in warm weather I suspect the reason became obvious. The EC down the Back Fold was used by five cottages – and any of us children who wanted to go when out at play. It had a wide wooden seat with two circular holes cut in side by side – two people could go simultaneously – and there were two wooden lids to cover the holes. Hanging behind the door, on a piece of string, were newspaper squares. Toilet rolls were unheard of. The EC was a draughty, smelly place and you never lingered there. It was not unusual, on a windy day, to use the newspaper, drop it in the hole and have it blown back in your face. The old EC at Granny Hayto's house in the village hadn't been used for years. My father grew rhubarb and mushrooms in it. We had bumper crops! The Elsan closet was a bucket with disinfectant in the bottom which fitted into an outer casing with a proper lavatory seat but it was still outside, down the garden path. I hated to go after dark in the winter. It was spooky, even though we had a torch or a lantern. Everyone had a guzunda (chamber-pot) under the bed.

Several years ago I was teaching a group of children an old song about wash-day. It began on Monday and progressed through the week to Sunday when we 'wore our linen-o'. The word mangle occurred. One child asked me what a mangle was! I must admit this question stopped me in my tracks, until the realization dawned that today's children won't know about mangling the washing as all they ever see is the laundry going round and round in a machine. How different from my experiences at the same age.

Wash-day was always Monday, but began on Sunday night by filling the copper built into the corner of the scullery with cold water and lighting the fire underneath so there would be hot water for Monday's early start. Whenever the weather was fine it was done outside, even in winter. We had several dolly tubs, a ponch and a dolly peg, as well as the mangle. This was an enormous thing with big wooden rollers which lived permanently outside. The washing was taken from the tub standing in front of it and, after a good ponching and dollying, mangled through into another tub standing behind it holding the rinsing water. Here everything was rinsed and mangled again before pegging out to dry. All white cottons were boiled in the copper before ponching and rinsing in water which had been 'blued'. The 'blue bag' cost a penny. It was swished round in the rinsing water until it looked blue enough. Use too much and all your whites were pale blues. Incidentally, the blue bag was the standard remedy for wasp stings. It worked like magic. Throughout the washing, the copper was kept stoked and topped up with cold water for a constant supply of hot water. Our ponch was thin copper rather like an upturned colander on a long pole. You had to pound the washing with it. The dolly peg was like a four-legged stool made of wood, with a pole rising from the middle. The dolly peg had to be twisted clockwise and anti-clockwise in the washing. Stubborn stains were given extra rubbing with carbolic soap and a brush. Detergents were not invented but soap powders were on the market. I seem to recall Rinso and Oxydol and Lux Flakes for hand washing.

I used to enjoy wash-day, but I doubt whether my mother and granny did. It was jolly hard work.

In 1938 my father changed his work location. He'd been at Miller's Dale station for £2 5s per week for a number of years. He got a job as a shunter at Rowsley sidings. Better pay, but it was shift work. He travelled on his motor bike but one winter was enough to persuade him that the journey, plus the shift work, was not feasible, especially when he had two bad attacks of bronchitis. Since both sets of grandparents were now dead, there was nothing to keep us in Hucklow, so Mum and Dad bought a brand new house at Northwood Lane only a quarter of a mile from Dad's work. We finally moved there in November 1939 thus severing our link with the village.

CHAPTER FOUR

A NORTHAMPTONSHIRE CHILDHOOD

Afflicted with polio at the age of thirteen months, Mrs Elsie Routh describes her struggle to live a normal life as a child in a small Northamptonshire village in the 1920s.

My maiden name was Wilson and I was born on 12 August 1912, in the village of Loddington, in Northamptonshire, 15 miles from Northampton and 5 miles from Kettering, which was our shopping town. There were no buses, so unless you could cadge a lift you walked; it was the only way of getting to Kettering or any surrounding district.

I am the only surviving member of my family out of three boys and five girls. The boys went on to the farm and the girls into domestic service except for me. Before my mother married she was in domestic service. My father was a horse-keeper for the biggest farmer in Loddington. We had our own farm outside the village in another small place, but the farm where my father worked was a large one. At one time he had ten horses, so you can judge the size of the farm as well as the one Dad worked on in the village.

I didn't go out to domestic work as unfortunately I had polio at the age of thirteen months. I walked for six weeks and then I developed polio, at that time it was called infantile paralysis. The rest of the family weren't isolated, because at that time two or three of my brothers and sisters were married. I was born when Mother was forty and Dad was forty-eight, so I never knew young parents. I wasn't operated on till I was three. I was lucky I got away with just the left leg and thigh but it blighted my life really. I was determined it would not make any difference to the jobs I had and I wouldn't give up anything. Later I worked as a tailoress in a factory, K.C. Clothing Factory, Kettering, as at that time the buses had just started to run. I started work when I was fourteen-and-a-half and I retired in 1937 to look after my ailing mother. She had heart trouble for twenty-two years.

In my young days the village children played various games such as whipping top and skipping. I could skip, I could play whipping top and I could play marbles. With whipping top you just had a bit of leather or string, which was wound round a top. Some of the tops used to have a Peggy Top, like a leg to it, the others were more of a solid piece of wood with the string round the top and you let it spin and you kept whipping it up so it went on for a long time. We used to play hide and seek, which I enjoyed, but when there were any team games they always dithered about choosing me in their team. I was always left to the last. I was very timid in those days. We usually played rounders but sometimes something different cropped up. There were about fifty children in the village at that time running wild.

In those days some of the children had bread and jam or bread and dripping. I know one family had bread and lard and sugar to eat but we never did. We had milk from the farm where Dad worked. I should say we had a quart a day and we used to fetch it in a can from the farm. Mother used to put it in a big bowl and skim the top and save it and then we used to shake it up in a can and sometimes it took hours to separate the cream from the milk. Eventually it did come into a big blob of butter. Mother then mixed a bit of salt in with it, patted it and made it look like a slab of butter you bought from a shop, because there were no shops you could go to buy any.

We only had a village post office which was on the main street, where they used to sell everything from pegs to pots. There was no electricity in those days so the shop sold candles too.

It also sold stamps, writing paper and envelopes and I remember we used to get boiled sweets, they didn't have Mars Bars or anything like that in those days. I suppose you could buy a slab of chocolate but I don't remember having any. I can only remember the boiled sweets but not a lot because mother couldn't afford to pay for them often.

There was a man who visited from Rothwell 2 miles away in his van. There was always someone coming round with odds and ends, so you didn't have to go to the shops to get them. I suppose you would call them tinkers – they had everything. We used to open the door and they would say 'Oil or anything'. The man from Rothwell had soap. I suppose there were some types of powder but I can only remember White Windsor soap.

The wages my father got were very small. I know he was working and I cannot remember him having less than 29s shillings a week but I think he must have done in my earlier memory. He earned £1 9s 0d for a week's work and he was up at 5 o'clock in the morning, going along to the farm, giving the horses their breakfast and then coming back and having his own at about 6 o'clock. By then mother would be up and have the kettle boiling. In those days you couldn't switch on, you had to light a fire and sometimes if the sticks were a bit damp it was 'hell on earth'. The sticks were placed in the oven overnight so that they were dry ready for the early start. If Dad was up, Mother got up as well. Dad had his breakfast and then it was our turn to get up.

Dad's day would really start after he had finished his breakfast at 7 o'clock. He looked after the horses which had to be mucked out. There was a big yard where they held all the horses' muck, the manure, as they couldn't cart it away every day. They were big shire horses he had to handle and he loved it. He was the head horse-keeper, which was a very important job in those days because there were no tractors and everything was done by horse power. One side of the square the farmer kept pigs. He was the biggest farmer in the area. I never saw him with his coat off doing any work. He was always like a gentleman but him and Dad got on ever so well. It was always George and 'the boss' and although they were two men, he was always the boss and Dad called him the boss.

I started attending school when I was five, which was a bit late because I had my operation when I was three. The doctor who did the operation split a guide at the back of my leg and made it into two. He said it would never be the same as the other leg, but it would be better. It was, so I progressed and I have tried to live a normal life never using that as an excuse. I always wanted to be the same as other people and not be different, so I have fought it all my life.

In the school building there were only two rooms, an infants' room and a larger room for up to standard five or six. The headmistress had this end of the school as her room, the junior school end. The infants' room was separated and we only had the door open there for assembly. It was and still is a wonderful building. It has been improved recently with school dinners and other amenities but it is still a beautiful school.

My first memory of the infant school was being given a strip of glossy leather with eyelets in to teach you how to lace your shoes up. Of course we had lace-up boots then, or button boots, although I never had a pair of them. The girls all wore knitted socks, some of them came up above the knee. My mother knitted mine but all the girls were taught to knit on four needles. I remember the number of stitches now and turning the heel and down to the toes.

Just after the war ended a Major Brooks-Banks came to live at Loddington in one of the big houses, along with his batman. He had a family of five children. This introduced more children into the school. Mrs Brooks-Banks had lovely ideas for us Loddington children and she worked so hard. She introduced the Brownies to the village and then from Brownies we graduated to Girl Guides.

The Major introduced Scouts to the village and also the Cubs, so there was something for the boys and girls to do. I learnt more from going in for badges. As I couldn't walk like the others I was so interested in getting these badges, acquiring as many as I could. We also went on camps, but only one day camps as there were no buses and few trains. Mrs Brooks-Banks did much to enlarge our minds and our lives. In 1924 Mrs Midgeley was instituted into the village school as headmistress. She came from Leeds having been educated there. She was quite a formidable lady but we kept friends all her life. When Mrs Midgeley arrived she rather resented these Brownie and Scout activities. I think she thought they would take some of her glory away.

At one time I was going backwards and forwards to Northampton hospital because of my illness. Mother used to have to go and plead to anyone who was a JP, or who subscribed to the hospitals, for a letter to keep on with the treatment I was having. I had to see the doctor very often to see how my leg was going on and these letters, for which my mother had to more or less go 'cap in hand' to get me free treatment, were important otherwise I would have ended up as a cripple. Of course my mother and father couldn't afford to pay for the treatment. Northampton hospital, where the doctor did my operation, was 15 miles away and how Mother ever got there I do not know. The doctor had to go in to the Army during the First World War but when he was on leave he used to send cards out to his patients to come and see him to see how they were getting on.

By this time the farmer had acquired a car and when he went to Northampton market he used to take Mother and me and drop us in the town so we could attend the hospital for observation. I was in plaster for two years so I used to go every fortnight, and the year after every month, so it was a struggle. I think there was a bus that ran between Kettering and Northampton but mother would have to get to Broughton, which was nearer than Kettering, up and down hills, which was a long way. She would have to take me in a folding pusher which went on the rack in the bus, if it didn't fall off! The farmer's car we went in was a Ford. It had a canvas top and it was cold before we had the side bits on. Often he used to stop and have a drink and it was so cold waiting. Mother was always prepared to stop in the hospital as there was a cup of tea and a currant bun, but there was nothing else available as there often is today. We used to sit there in the warm until the farmer came back from the sales because that is where he did his marketing.

Some years later Sir Harry Mansfield bequeathed a large house for use as an orthopaedic hospital and clinics were formed in various places. I went to Northampton first and then Wellingborough as by then the buses had started. It must have been in the 1920s as it was before I was twelve. We had to walk to catch a bus as we were rather isolated. It was the squire's daughter, Mary Steel, who had been a nurse in the war, who initially encouraged me to go to this clinic and become a member of the Northamptonshire Orthopaedic Clinic Society, and I attended this clinic up to 1946. By then I think they thought they had done all they could for me apart from letting me have the surgical boots that I always had to wear. I was therefore counselled out but I always had my shoes free. I got my shoes through the Northampton Crippled Children's Society and I was always grateful to them. I was a big girl then by 1946!

One of my favourite pastimes before I was twelve was to watch the men cleaning the wheat that had been in the sacks in the big barn ready for transit or re-cropping the fields. Before they did that, they had to dress it and this was what fascinated me. They used to tip the sacks of corn on to the stone floor and then shovel it about. When they were dressing the corn they used a dressing called Aldren. It was a preservative so that the seed corn was good. Eventually they had to pack up dressing the corn with Aldren because it killed so many birds. If any of the hens ate any of this dressed corn it poisoned them but I loved to watch the dressing being done. The corn was stored in the barn until they took it to

Lamport or Kettering stations. God help you if you were in the way when the wagons were on the move. It was a day's work to go to Lamport and the men's tempers were a bit frayed.

The only thing we children had to look forward to was the chapel tea at Rothwell and we were taken any way we could get there. This tea party was always held in July but there wasn't one for the church children. Unfortunately the chapel closed at the end of the last war.

I was getting towards the age of twelve when my sister Clara was killed by a car when she was fetching water from the village pump which was half-way down the street. Mum and Dad were upset because Clara was killed on her bike, so that was out for the time being. Eventually they did succumb and I had a Standard bicycle with a raised pedal on the left side; a firm in Kettering made it.

I had an extra term at school because I hadn't got a job. I used to sit doing fancy work, like making tablecloths. Mrs Midgeley, the teacher, taught me a lot of different stitches, which I loved doing. I was really her general dogsbody, as I always kept her desk and other bits and pieces like that tidy, which I was intrigued to do.

In the middle of the next term, before my birthday, I had a job at the shoe factory in Rothwell. I worked for seven months in the factory, in the closing room, earning 7s a week. This factory is still going today, the only one left in the town out of the seven there were then. My job was to stick supports on where the eyelets were. A lot of men had boots which had three eyelets at the top; they laced up to these eyelets and used these eyelets to finish off with. Then I had to stick what they called staybits on the boots and stick in the loops on the back for machining. (These were loops with the size and the name of the firm on.) They pulled the boots on with these loops. I didn't really like the work as I always wanted to get into clothing and I had my name down to get a job with K.C. Clothing.

I think they were a bit hesitant because of my foot on the machine pedal, and so instead I was given a tacking job. This operation was 'based on facings'; the lining was tacked on to the main body of the coat after it had been paired with the proper size collar and lapels. This was a slightly more experienced job; while I was waiting for work, I did sleeve headings. I was paid about 7s 9d per week.

Around that time the buses, run by a private firm, had started so I had transport to Kettering. The fare was 2s 6d per week which had to come out of my wages. At that time all I wanted to do was to save up £100 and to make my mother a new winter coat as she had never had one in my memory. I was on what they called 'piece/daywork'. What we didn't do one month we worked the next month, so it was evened out. Some girls were earning more than I was, as I was always a bit on the slow side but they said I was thorough. I must say that 27s 6d was the minimum and if you didn't do enough to earn that, then you had to pay it back. Some girls owed pounds. The firm had to pay them 27s 6d but after that, if they didn't earn it, the girls had to pay the firm back. They didn't have a rise until they had paid it back. We had to buy our own cottons and tacking threads and the girls on machines had to pay for machine threads. There were then over a thousand girls working there and to think it all dwindled away to nothing. They did give us a bit of bonus for earning over a pound, but it was only 1s 3d in the pound and I didn't have a cent back. I worked there for ten years and, in the end, the company went bankrupt. I had left before then to look after Mother.

In 1924, just before my sister was killed, we had a crystal set radio. You had to turn a knob and find a spot on the crystal inside, there wasn't much mechanism to it. My dad used to love that crystal set, especially when he had the earphones on and Henry Hall was playing with his band. We only had one pair of earphones and we all had to share them. We used to sit close together so we could all hear through one of the earphones. The people at the hall were still there at this time and they had a great big wireless with a big horn and people used to go up there after church and chapel were over on Sundays and listen when there was a service on the wireless.

In those days there was nothing much to do; a man could go to the pub and we went for walks. A woman wouldn't dream of going into a pub. My brother didn't smoke until he was about twenty and as for having a glass of beer, it was out of the question. They were still considered boys at that age. You weren't grown up like you are today. You had to be twenty-one before you were considered grown up whereas nowadays it is much earlier. It was quite exciting in those times, however, because there were so many new inventions.

CHAPTER FIVE

GROWING UP IN THE FENS

We go now to the fen country of Cambridgeshire, to what was known at that time as the Isle of Ely, to hear the story of Mr Wilfred George Ling.

I was born in Ringsfield, Suffolk on 20 March 1921. My father was a soldier returned from the First World War, having spent most of the war in the trenches. He was there at the age of seventeen and returned from the war to find that he had no job. He got married to my mother, who was the daughter of a farmworker. They had no home or money so they lived with my grandparents. I was born and I believe they were very poverty stricken. In fact, my mother once showed me some clothes I wore as a baby and they were literally patches on patches and this was fairly common at the time.

My father was apprenticed to a harness-maker in Saxmundham, pre-war, and I don't believe he returned there after the war. After some time being unemployed, he was fortunate to secure a post as a harness-maker on an estate in Cambridgeshire which belonged to the Co-operative Wholesale Society. He was in charge of the harness and the canvasses for the machinery which reaped the corn in those days, the binder, two hundred horses and, in addition, he was sometimes the chauffeur to the manager, who took the place of the village squire. He also did some of the kitchen garden but with two hundred horses' harnesses to look after there wasn't a lot of time for that.

My mother, when she could, did seasonal work on the land, potato picking and hoeing sugar beet, things like this. It was very hard for women in those days because there were no labour-saving gadgets. They had to do all the washing by hand; they did all the cooking; they had to fetch all the groceries very often from a town far away; they had to get the children off to school. They really worked very hard. They worked from 8 o'clock in the morning to 3 o'clock in the afternoon in the fields with only a half-an-hour's break for lunch. The work, particularly potato picking, was really back-breaking and it was a kind of slavery because they were terribly desperate to have the work and this was exploited. There were gang-masters in those days who took charge of this sort of labour and they really exploited the women and they worked very hard for just a few shillings a week. Nevertheless, this made a difference between just a subsistence living and living at a slightly better rate. So that was my very early beginning.

My earliest recollections are of where we lived at Coldham. I have no recollection of Suffolk because we moved to Coldham Co-op Estate in 1923. We lived in a four-roomed cottage which was accessed by a footpath over a grass field. There was a garden fence around it and just inside the garden gate was the cold water tap which was our source of supply. Most people had to have roof water, which was collected off the roofs in a cistern, but we were lucky as we were quite close to the farm buildings and could use the tap. Most people had a cistern which was a brick-built tank somewhere near the back door with a lid on it. People got water from the cistern with a bucket on a stick with a hook on it called a 'cistern hook' and I have one to this day hanging in a shed somewhere. There was a superstition that if you kept a newt in the cistern it kept the water clean and most cisterns had a newt in it and the water was often drunk unboiled. I didn't know anyone to have any serious effects so perhaps the newts were effective.

Inside the back door of our house was the scullery. This was a little lean-to place built on to the main four rooms and in it was an old Dutch oven which had been used for making bread, which mother rarely used. There was a coal-fired copper for boiling the clothes. In later days I remember Mother sometimes cooked on a paraffin stove, which also stood in there. Just behind the door there was a little table with a bowl on it in which we washed with the soap and flannel on a dish beside it. A towel hung behind the door and under the table was a bucket for the dirty water. The dirty water was then taken down the garden and flung into a ditch. We had water in at the front door through the tap and like everybody else we got rid of the dirty water by just throwing it out. Those were the ablutions.

Inside the door in the main part of the house was the kitchen which had an old side oven (coal fired, of course) which worked or didn't depending on which way the wind was blowing and there Mother cooked and we had our meals. Then there was the parlour which, in my very earliest recollections, had no furniture in it because we didn't have any furniture for it. However, this was a parlour which was little used even when it was furnished; it was there for high days and holidays. Up the stairs was the main bedroom where my mother and father slept. It had a lean-to roof and access to my bedroom was through this room which again was a little lean-to bedroom. That was all there was to the house but it was a pretty sound brick built house with a slate roof and it was home. It was very damp because there was no damp-proofing on the brick floors in those days. The best floor covering we could afford, and the only practical one, was linoleum which stayed there for a year or two before it rotted and which took a lot of polishing and keeping clean.

The lavatory in those days was a 'privy' down the garden – a brick built privy with a two-seater seat inside. One seat was for adults and one for children. The two seats were arranged over a vault which had to be emptied through a door in the back, perhaps once a year; a nasty smelly sort of a place but that is all there was in those days. Toilet paper was newspaper which was very often torn up and hung on a nail behind the door. I always remember people used to say in those days that it was the most appropriate use for the *News of the World*! So that was the house and the loo and it was surrounded by a garden. Dad being a keen gardener he grew all the vegetables we needed. In later years they kept a few chickens and at one time Dad kept a couple of pigs because pigs could be sold at Christmas time and there was a little extra money that way. But the whole thing was a very severe grind, there was very little relaxation. There was no radio. I remember the first radio we had was when I was quite a big lad. It was a second-hand radio and I am sure it was called a Red Star. It had a metal horn speaker and I thought it was quite remarkable to hear voices from outer space on this.

We went to town to do the shopping on a Saturday. The town was Wisbech, which was 7 miles away and we had to bike there. Mum had a box on the back of her bike in which I sat and we used to go to town to do the main shopping. Sometimes we used to go to March which was a bit nearer, about 4 miles away. Wisbech, I always remember, had stalls where Mum used to buy the meat. Very often it was an open stall. She used to bring the meat home wrapped up in newspaper. I remember the hard work the stall holders used to put in in those days, selling oranges, bananas and other things very cheaply compared with now. You could get sixty oranges I believe for a shilling and that shilling took a lot of earning. We didn't have a lot of luxuries but on rare occasions we had a few sweets. Twice a year there was a highlight when the Statute Fairs came to Wisbech. They were the old Hiring Fairs, although not used as hiring fairs in those days. I think that had finished before my time. The fairs still came, as they still do, and it was a very thrilling sight to see all the amusements going and the old steam engines chuffing away. One side of the market-place was taken up with a line of steam-engines. I can remember them clearly and I am still fascinated by steam-engines when they are preserved.

As well as shopping in Wisbech or March we had a baker call twice a week at the house. He came in a horse and cart. A butcher came in later days from March, again with a horse and cart. Later still groceries were delivered to the house by the local Co-op. In all these cases these tradesmen had to traipse across the footpath to our house, which was a couple of hundred yards. I don't think they were too pleased with that but like everybody else I suppose they were so pleased to earn a pound or even only a few coppers they didn't mind tramping across the field for our custom. Coal was delivered the same way. Paraffin we sometimes had delivered, but very often we fetched it from the nearest village. And, of course, when radio came along there were the old accumulators to be charged up which, with luck, would last a week. We had two accumulators, one being charged and one in use. That was about all the entertainment we ever had.

I remember very clearly Mum taking me to the fruit fields in the summer-time to earn money that way. Wisbech was a very big fruit growing district and still is. In those days its economy was largely based on the strawberry; the jam factories were there, the places for making the baskets used when the strawberries were picked and sold, tools for cultivating the strawberries and just about everything. It made Wisbech a fairly prosperous town in those days compared with everywhere else. It was also a place where there was always a bit of casual work to be had and so there were always casual workers coming around in the fruit picking time. You couldn't find a spare corner that didn't have a gypsy caravan parked on it. Tramps came from all around the country just to earn a few shillings and the local people had to compete with these to get a bit of extra pocket-money.

I can remember the fruit fields were about 2 to 3 miles from where we lived. My mother sometimes got a lift there with a horse and cart and once the horse and cart that took them there in the morning didn't turn up. She often told me in later years she did a day's work in the fruit fields and then carried me 3 miles home. My own recollection of it is going there on the back of her bike in this box contraption that Dad made and she would stay in the fruit fields picking strawberries and gooseberries all day long and go home at night back to the grind of housework.

I remember well the women in the fields picking the fruit, and planting and picking the potatoes. It was the custom in the Fens in those days and Coldham was on the brinks of the Fens. I think they called it 'skirtland', being on the very edge of the Fens. All the women wore bonnets with a hood over the front stiffened with a piece of cane, which stuck out in front of the face about 4 inches. The bonnets also had a bit hanging down the nape of the neck to protect the wearer from the sun and the dust. The women wore the usual heavy clothes in those days, long skirts, sometimes canvas or hessian aprons, and sometimes nice, clean, white cotton aprons. They made a quite colourful sight. They were all very hard-working, and hard times I am afraid made hard people and they weren't above doing each other down to get an extra shilling for themselves. Most of them, however, were comradely and took care of one another.

I should have mentioned that most of the work done by the women, fruit picking, potato picking and planting potatoes, was piece-work, which meant they got paid by results which made it all the harder. Most work in those days in the labour intensive jobs was piece-work and people worked very hard and got in the habit of working very hard and they actually 'ran' at their work and I'm afraid to this day I still run. I run down the garden to do this or that and I trot back again. It doesn't do me any good but it is a habit. That is my earliest recollection of work and most of my childhood. In spite of not having any money or recreation or very many friends, there were very few of us down there as children, looking back some of us agree we had a privileged childhood. Although we had hardly anything except just enough food, just enough clothes to get by, we had one thing that the children of this day and age just have not got. We had space – thousands of acres on which to roam around. Of course, we did no damage, we understood the countryside, nobody bothered about us walking across fields and we could walk where we wanted. Nature was an open book to us. There were thousands of birds and we knew them all. We collected one egg from every nest we could until we had a great big collection of birds' eggs, quite illegal now of course and properly so. There were still snakes to be found, grass snakes and the adder I remember. There were thousands of rabbits of all kinds in some of the grassland and rooks by the thousand. We could climb the trees and get to the rooks' nests. There were also pigeons, magpies, jays, hawks; we knew many trees that had owls' nests in. Looking back we weren't as fortunate as maybe it seemed.

At harvest time, when I was about twelve, we could sometimes get a job leading the horses. We led the horses down the field with an empty wagon and led it back again with a loaded one to the stack. We worked every hour there was. We didn't work Sundays in those days but we did work Saturday afternoons and we worked every hour of daylight, about sixty hours, for the magnificent sum of 12s a week, which is 60p nowadays. Anyway, it was a great thrill to do a little work and at a very early age I learned to work with horses. I also learned the craft of building stacks and a lot about land work.

One of the things that sticks in my mind about harvest is that, about a week before, all the men used to have white calico patches sewn on to their trousers' knees and on the elbows of their jackets in anticipation of the work that was coming. Harvest work with sheaves was very hard on the clothes. If you had a decent pair of trousers, in no time you wore the knees out and you couldn't afford to do this. Before harvest, then, all the wives got to work and sewed calico patches on all of the men's trousers just above the knees to half-way down the shin and so everybody could be seen cycling to work with these white patches on their trousers. I remember that very well and, of course, by the end of the harvest the patches were worn through but the trousers underneath were at least saved in part. Also people wore good leather boots in those days, before the days of wellingtons. They say there was no such thing as waterproof boots but these boots were waterproof. They were kept waterproofed with goose fat. Looking back, one of the things that has made life in the countryside more bearable, second only to the motor car, is the wellington boot. Our boots were very hard and often uncomfortable to wear and eventually they did leak. You couldn't afford to throw them away when they first leaked so you wore them until they were really worn out and there was always a period when you had wet and cold feet.

The school I attended was a Church of England school and it was about 1¼ miles from where I lived. I walked there in the morning and we had our lessons and we walked back again. It was a strange school by today's standards. There were just two rooms and there were three teachers teaching all age groups from five to fourteen in these two rooms. You can imagine it was pretty hectic in the biggest room which had two classes going in it. Nevertheless, this was all the schooling we had and there were none of the teaching aids of today and we learnt our times tables by chanting them. We learned arithmetic and we became reasonably good at English. It was a very elementary primary education but it was all there was and we did reasonably well on it. I only knew one fellow who left school not being able to read and write and I suppose in this day and age he might have been called dyslexic. So everybody I knew left school, got a job and brought up a family. Many of them acquitted themselves very well in the war and became business people.

The school itself was brick with a slate roof. There was just one water tap over a sink in a sort of scullery place. There were brick lavatories again with a vault underneath, two for boys and two for girls. The boys had in addition a urinal outside of the main lavatories with a six foot wall around it. One of the things that makes me chuckle now is the thought that there used to be competitions to see which boy could 'pee' over the top of this wall and some of them could. When the wind was in the wrong direction I think that is what coined the phrase 'getting your own back'! I sometimes see the champion now. He is an old man who was crippled on the convoys into Russia in the war. I sometimes wonder if he remembers when he was the champion at 'peeing over the wall'.

There was no dining-room in the school and, of course, we took our own packed lunches which were sandwiches of sorts wrapped in newspaper. There wasn't much paper to be had in those days and you wouldn't get proper paper for packing lunches. As there was nowhere to eat them we sat outside in the playground with our backs to whatever wall protected us best from the wind or the sun as the case might be. There was just a gravel yard, very small, and we couldn't play many games in there except the sort of games which are no longer played like 'ring of roses'. The main road ran by, a tarmac road which was fairly unique in those days. We used to play with whips and tops and hoops on there and if it froze hard in the winter, as it did, we could make slides on the road. We used to make some good slides. One of the other pastimes was to go out of the playground up the road to where some of the farm ditches were. In the Fens, of course, there were very few hedges. The fields are intersected by ditches instead, and one of our games was jumping these ditches. Sometimes, of course, somebody jumped in which made it all the more interesting.

We did a bit of bird nesting in the dinner hour but I can't remember all the things we did. We loafed around and played our games, and fights were just a bit of a pastime too. The girls rather kept to themselves and did girlish things. There were always tramps coming by. We used to watch them come by sometimes with a good deal of apprehension. Horses and carts used to pass by on the way to the station with loads of corn or potatoes or whatever. When horses were the only power on the land we used to watch out for the turnout in the way the brasses were polished and the amount of ribbons and braid used on the horses' manes and tails and so on and comment on this. Occasionally the old steam-engines would come by or a steam-wagon. We weren't far off the railway line and we would watch the trains go by and wonder where they went.

Actually, I was one of the few people who ever went on a train. My grandparents still lived in Suffolk and at Christmas my parents and I would spend one year with my mother's people and the next year with my father's people and so on. So I still kept some touch with Suffolk.

So that was school. The teachers were women and they biked, believe it or not, right from Wisbech or March. The head teacher was a Mrs Shanks and I remember her coming all the way from Wisbech on this sit-up-and-beg bike. I remember her arriving and she was a bit of a martinet but she was a very good teacher really. She did a good job with what she had. Some of the younger teachers had motor bikes. The buses then hadn't started to run and although the station was only half a mile away the trains weren't at the right time and maybe they couldn't afford the trains anyway. There was a bell at the school which used to be rung and, being a Church school, the rector used to come and give us scripture lessons and he was a bit of a tyrant, worse than the teachers. If you didn't sit up and take notice you got a clip on the ear from him. Not a very Christian man, I don't think, but they were very much the same in those days!

We had a school garden which the estate let us have, about half an acre of land. If the teachers got fed up with us in class they sent us out to garden, sometimes in all weathers. We dug the garden and planted things, and learnt to garden at a very early age. There was no transport to or from the school. Some children walked perhaps 3 or 4 miles to get there, often across fields until they got to the road. Absenteeism, because of sickness, was fairly common but it was quite uncommon for children to be absent for any other reason. They got to school somehow and they must have walked probably for an hour and a quarter to get there. I am quite sure some of them did and they did it twice a day, every day.

Holidays were the highlights of course. Like everybody else, we didn't like school that much and we didn't want to stay there all the year round.

Eventually I left school at the age of fourteen without any qualifications. There were no certificates to be handed out. There was a scholarship to go to the Grammar School, which I could have won, I suppose, but there were only about a dozen scholarship places in the whole of the county and I didn't get one of them. So I left school with nothing for it, and with no job. I wanted to get in to engineering and I biked for miles and miles around every engineering place I could find in the whole district and there was nothing doing. Very often one wouldn't even get an interview. There was no dole money, of course and boys and girls leaving school had to be supported by their parents. It was a bleak outlook and I have never forgotten going to one man called Bodger, who was an engineer in Wisbech. I stood in front of him, took my hat off very respectfully as my mother had taught me and said, 'Please Sir, do you have a vacancy for a boy?' He looked at me and said, 'I have got too many like you now' and he just turned and walked away. I have employed scores and scores of people myself since then and if ever anyone came to me asking for a job and I couldn't use them, I always said, 'No I am sorry, I don't have a job because . . . ', and I always explained why I didn't have a job.

CHAPTER SIX

MEMORIES OF A GLOUCESTERSHIRE GIRL

From Gloucestershire I received this account in 1988 of the early experiences of Mrs Patricia Gould who was born on 29 September 1922 at Littleton-upon-Severn.

Father was a winchman at the local brick and tile works. In the village there was a school and a small Ebenezer chapel. The school was more or less central. It had a very small playground and there were only about twenty pupils, but even then we had an infant school with a teacher in one separate building linked with a little passageway to a larger building where all the other children stayed until they were fourteen. There were two teachers, one in charge of each section. The church was in the middle of the village. We had a rector with a nice big rectory and in the summer there would be the rectory fête or the church fête which was quite an event.

We lived in a little house which was the end of a terrace, a stone house, and although it was quite attractive with large sash windows, it had stone floors and was very damp, consequently we suffered quite a lot of ill health. The village was quite a happy community. We had many little functions. There was the school concert and then the older people had singing evenings or community singing. We had most things delivered to the village because the only shop was a very small corner shop which belonged to a lady whose husband had a small-holding and she would sell a few basics. I remember going to get the milk with a little milk-can, with a lid on it. The thing was we tried to swing it round and round as fast as we could without the milk coming out. I am afraid there were a few accidents at times.

The postman was a fairy godfather in lots of ways. He would bring different bits of shopping from Thornbury which was about 5 miles away. We had no bus, of course, in those days and no motor cars. If we wanted to go to Bristol we would have to walk either to Thornbury or in the other direction about another 5 miles to pick up the bus from Pilning to Bristol. A lady started a kind of taxi service which ran about once a week. She would come out and take some of the housewives who wanted to go to Bristol for shopping. The rector's wife had a pony trap. Sometimes she would take my mother shopping to Thornbury. She was a very nice lady. Among the things the postman brought were items such as ladies' corsets. We had two bakers delivering in the village from the next larger village which was Olveston. They had those old-fashioned bakers' carts. We also had a butcher delivering with his cart which was a special kind, not refrigerated as I don't think they had ice in those days but it was all very hygienic and clean with a lid. Later the milk was brought round in cans but when I was young I had to collect it.

The pub was a haven for most of the men. On a Sunday morning I went to Sunday school before the church service. Then there was the morning service and in the afternoon we had Sunday school in the school. The church was a little walk away and then again there would be evening service. In summer-time the usual thing was to go for a walk after church. If it was really nice we would walk down to the Severn and sit on the bank and meet up with different people, or maybe just have a good walk around the village. The village is not the same now. All the cottages have been bought by people with a lot of money and they have been made into little palaces almost. The rectory has been sold off, there is just a visiting rector or vicar who looks after several villages, coming to them in turn.

In the summer we would help with the farm work. Everyone would go to the haymaking fields, and the farmers were all friendly. I remember picking dandelions earlier on for my mother to make dandelion wine. Another thing we did in the spring was to go to the woods and collect primroses and decorate the church for Easter. In the autumn there were plenty of hazelnuts to be picked. We would go for picnics on the Severn bank. It was a very muddy river so it usually meant a bath when we got home if we had been paddling around in it.

My worst memories about life at Littleton were when my mother was ill in hospital. My grandmother helped to look after me and she lived in a house which was quite isolated. We had to go down a lane which was very muddy in the winter and then go across three fields and up an orchard to get to the house. I was only about seven this particular occasion when I was staying with her and I had to go there for my lunch because there was no such thing as school dinners, not even hot milk. My grandmother had a little fox terrier and he would come to meet me but unfortunately he chased the cows. I would get to the stile and think 'I hope Tracker isn't there' because when Tracker chased the cows I couldn't run as fast as the dog and the cows very often finished up between me and the stile. If I thought the cows might be there then I would go down the lane and I would be scared of snakes. I was only quite little then and all by myself. I think that my father decided the next time my mother went to hospital I had better stay at home and he would look after me. She was often in hospital as her health was very bad. Eventually she developed TB, but we were happy and she was very modern. She still is. She is eighty-seven now and she still likes to look nice. In those days she would keep up as well as she could with fashion and in the 1920s she wore short dresses and had her hair cut with a bob and fringe. My mother always dressed me nicely. She had an eye for colour and fashion. My grandmother was a very good needlewoman and she would make me nice velvet or silk dresses with smocking, honeycombing and that kind of thing.

We were the first people in the village to have a wireless with earphones and we also had a gramophone before any one else. I remember the records 'Ramona', 'My Blue Heaven' and 'Bye Bye Blackbird'. We read a lot too. I suppose being an only child my books were my life. My grandmother had quite a good selection of books. She was quite well educated. Her people were Bristolian business people and she had married a farmer. Unfortunately, although he owned his own farm and was a not a tenant farmer, he was a drunkard. He drank and gambled, everything was lost and he finished up more or less working for anything or anybody. But my grandmother was very fond of books and I suppose we inherited that love.

I left Littleton when I was nine. We moved away from there and I stayed with my grandmother. I read *She* by Rider Haggard, *Pilgrim's Progress* – anything she had, I would read. I was always bought books for birthdays and Christmas.

The water supply at Littleton was very poor. There was a well at the bottom of the village and I remember my father getting the water in buckets on a 'yoke', a wooden bar that goes across the shoulders with buckets suspended on chains each side. That water was used for drinking. We did have a well, a rain-water well. Of course the lavatory was just an earth closet. We had quite a large garden and my father worked hard on this and on an allotment as well.

We had oil lamps and coal fires and candles. My mother would light a big copper for washing and get up early in the morning to get it going. She would wash and boil the clothes, rinse them, blue them, starch them, hang them out and get them in and then iron them. All had to be done and there seemed to be a competition between all the housewives as to who could get it out earlier than the others.

Some of the people, to help make ends meet, would foster children and there was a Waifs and Strays Society. My mother had a boy and a girl whose home had been burnt and they had been found on the road wandering with their father. They stayed with us for a few years. When they were about eleven or twelve they had to go away to the orphanage to be trained to earn their living. The girl was very close to us and she treated my mother as her mother. She called her 'Aunty' and we were like her family. We didn't hear much from the boy afterwards. I lost track of him and as my mother's health wasn't very good we didn't have anyone else. When the girl left the orphanage and went out to work she always came to us for her holidays and I was her bridesmaid when she got married. Unfortunately she died of cancer shortly after having a child. It seemed so tragic. It was quite accepted in the village that people would foster children. They called it 'boarding out' in those days.

I was very ill myself with pneumonia and chest conditions through bad housing and, of course, shortage of money. Also the house was low lying and obviously didn't suit us.

At school I remember the hounds coming by and we all ran out to watch them and I had the cane because I was one of the naughty ones who went to see them. These days I wouldn't go out of the house to watch hunting at all, having seen a kill close at hand.

My mother kept me dressed in a modern style. She was a good knitter and I remember she would knit me little suits. The skirts would be like a rib that looked pleated on a cotton bodice, with a jumper to match. There was one family in the village who were quite old-fashioned and the girls wore very beautifully starched embroidery pinafores with the frilled sleeves over their dresses and they always had long hair with bows in it. Of course, I had a bob with a fringe which was a typical 1920s style. I had an aunt who lived in London, a real 'Modern Millie' because she even had the 'shingle cut'.

My days at Littleton when I was young were quite happy ones. I cannot remember much hardship apart from when Mother was in hospital. The pub was kept by a farmer, most people seemed to do a couple of jobs, and it was quite a quiet one. He also kept some cows. He had a horse and every evening you could hear him going

The infant class at Littleton-upon-Severn C. of E. School, 1928–9 (Gould)

down the road on this horse, a strawberry-roan it was. He would say 'Gee-up! Whoa! Whoa! Gee-up!' It was like this all the time. Of course there were always plenty of cow pancakes down the road because cattle were taken backwards and forwards from the fields down through the village to the milking parlours.

Where my grandmother lived there were two large orchards and a lot of apples were used for cider. She didn't make cider herself but the cider-making farmers would collect them. Certain apples were cider apples, not the ordinary eating ones. They were very sharp. I remember the sweet ones, the eating ones, 'Morgan Sweets' and things like that. There was not even a well at my grandmother's house. They had to get the water from a stream. It was a nice house but very primitive from that point of view. They had lots of fruit, apples, apricots on the wall and a cherry tree. She kept hens in a large pen because there was plenty of land but when you fed them they would all fly up around you. I was terrified of them but I don't think she ever lost any to foxes. I never remember hearing of it anyway. I think foxes had plenty of rabbits in those days to keep them fed.

We used to go to the Severn and walk under the cliffs out to a large rock which when the tide went out left lots of pools and we would swim in these pools. There were stepping-stones over the mud to get to them as the Severn was and still is a very muddy river. It was quite an event to go down for a picnic by the Severn.

When I was nine, in 1932, we left Littleton and we moved to a house higher up on a hill, not very much further away, about 5 miles. Because the house was higher, it was healthier and my mother's health and mine improved and I grew quite strong. The house was in a sort of hamlet. There were no shops or anything – the nearest shop was 1½ or 2 miles away down in the main village where the school and church and everything else was.

I went to the school there which was a larger school altogether than Littleton. I could tell the difference when I got there as there was a large playground for boys and another large one for girls. It was in the shape of a cross as a lot of schools were. We had an infant teacher in the main room of the cross piece and that was where the assembly was held and then there was a class for the intermediate stages and then the scholarship class and the headmaster helped the top class. I was in a class of about forty pupils. The four boys the headmaster thought potential scholarship winners were in his class and he coached them on. Those four boys and I were the only ones who passed the scholarship in 1933 out of that huge class. The headmaster had told my mother I wouldn't pass the 'oral' but I did. When we got confirmation that I had acquired a free place, as they called it, we had a letter from the County Council saying I had this free place but if my father's wages went over a certain amount he would have to pay. Also they provided a bicycle because we lived 3 miles away from the school. The children who were on a bus route had a bus pass.

Things seemed to change quite considerably in the thirties. Life was much quicker than when we were at Littleton. It seemed as though we started to move at a much quicker pace. We had a bus then that ran from the village to Littleton and if we wanted to go Bristol we had two alternative routes. There was also a station at Thornbury by that time and we could travel either to Yate or to Gloucester, but this has been closed for many years now. The main village had quite a lot of facilities. There was a chapel, church, parish hall, a large school. The church was very large and we went to Sunday school as usual. Very often in the lunch hour from school we would go out and play in the fields of kale. This was, of course, before I went to the Grammar School.

I was only at Olveston School for about a year and I was very apprehensive at the thought of going to the Grammar School because I was the only girl going from the village. There were one or two who had gone there from previous years but of course they would be in higher classes anyway. I was granted a small amount each term by the County Council, about 13s I think it was, to help buy books and pencils and that kind of thing. My uniform was provided by the British Legion Benevolent Society. I think that is what they called it, because my father had been in the First World War and was a member of the British Legion. It was a great help because my parents had very little money. My father earned very little. Unfortunately the uniform was not exactly the same as that purchased in the local town, where we were supposed to buy it. Everything was just slightly different which marked us out as having British Legion uniforms, but even so we were very grateful to it because I don't think I could have gone otherwise. Quite a lot of the other children in the class were 'fee payers'. They had

The scholarship winners at Littleton-upon-Severn school, 1933

obtained a place, but not a free one. They had passed the scholarship but because they were the sons and daughters of the farmers or shopkeepers they would have to pay. There were other children in the B forms. They were also fee paying ones, mostly who were not very bright but whose parents could afford to pay for them to have a secondary education. Those of us who had won the scholarship purely on our merits had the free places, although it was a struggle. We used to work that bit harder I suppose because we knew how valuable it was. My mother knew the value of a good education because of her family's connections. Her cousins all went to good schools, so she was determined that I would have the chance.

It was a long ride in bad weather to the school and we were very often wet through when we got there, but it was a new school with central heating and nice cloakrooms where you could change into school shoes. We wore different shoes in the school to the ones we wore outside. We had quite a strict headmaster. It was a mixed school, which I think is a good thing. It also had a headmistress and the standard of education was pretty good. I had to stay at home quite a lot to look after my mother which reflected itself on my reports. 'She could do better if not so many absences', but that was how it was. My father could not stay away from work. If he had work he would go and if he was out of work, well that was that! Unfortunately as the thirties went on life got very hard. I had no pocket-money — there was no such thing as pocket-money. The fact that I had that education was the biggest sacrifice on my parents' part that could be imagined. I do not know how my mother managed to make ends meet. I remember just getting half a pint of milk a day from the milkman. We used to buy tinned milk. We grew everything in the garden we possibly could.

Life was very hard but at school I was happy. I kept in the A forms right the way through school. I was ten when I passed the scholarship and, as I was eleven shortly after, I started in the September. I took the School Certificate at fifteen, which is the equivalent of GCSEs today, and then I took a commercial course after that. Our house was a new council house built in 1932. Although it was new it had no electricity supply, just one tap in a sort of little scullery or kitchenette with a boiler and copper, and an outside toilet with a bucket. Eventually electricity was put in but bathing was still the same old ritual of heating up water for the tin bath. My father suffered. He had a hernia for years and he couldn't have an operation because he couldn't take time off from work to have it because the fact that he even had a job was so precious. He could be given his cards any time. It was a very precarious time. I remember my mother being ill once and the doctor said, 'Why didn't you send for me earlier?' She said, 'I was scared I couldn't pay the bill.' He said, 'Have I ever refused to come?' He was marvellous. She did manage to enrol me in a Friendly Society for which she paid a few pence a week so that if I was ill this would help to pay the doctor's bill. If we had anything seriously wrong with us and we had to see a specialist, we would be sent to the Bristol Royal Infirmary or the General Hospital, Bristol, which was very good. My mother had lots of operations. She needed to be in and out of hospital all of my life. Despite his hernia my father has kept very good health.

When we lived in the house at Littleton the cooking facilities consisted of an open fire. I suppose you would call it a hob fire with a little oven at the side. The cooking had to be done on that. Most people supplemented this with an oil stove. When we moved to the council house in Oldown there was a large cast-iron range, which was a great improvement. The room was at least warm and cooking could be done on the top and in the big oven at the side. It meant a lot of hard work though. The flues had to be cleaned once a week and of course it was all black-leaded. I remember my mother being quite black when she had finished and having to have a bath. Later on we had a primus stove, which was quite useful for frying and boiling a kettle quickly. Later in the thirties when we had electricity installed my mother and father managed to buy a small second-hand electric cooker. This made all the difference.

I remember also, when I was a child at Oldown in the thirties, seeing so many of the young men of the village who were out of work lounging around the football pitch on the green – nothing to do and no work. It was very depressing because it was a whole generation lost.

When we lived at Littleton I remember seeing the airship – the R 100 – passing over. We were very excited at seeing that. Of course later on when aircraft became more common we took it all for granted but the airship, of course, was something unique.

When I started at the Grammar School there were still no school dinners. We did have small beakers of Horlicks for a few pence a day. In around 1937–8 they did introduce school dinners consisting of a cooked meal and a pudding. This was 6d a day but very few could afford it. There was just one table for the élite, the rest of us took sandwiches. I think that we managed to afford for me to have cooked dinners about the last year I was there.

There were two school trips in the whole time I was at the Grammar School, which was about six years. One was to the theatre in Bristol to see *Twelfth Night* because we were studying this for the School Certificate. The other was to see some French films, I think one of them was *Mayerling* with Charles Boyer. They were trying to arrange a trip to Paris for the French class but unfortunately so few could afford it that it fell through.

We were very conscious of world affairs in the sixth form in 1938. We well remember Chamberlain, and Hitler's progress through Europe and how disgusted we felt that we didn't do anything about it. Of course we were mistaken as we realized later.

When we were at Olveston, of course, the school was larger as the village was larger and my circle of friends was different. There was quite a mixed community of farmers' daughters and sons and the local tailor's daughter was a great friend of mine. Until I passed the scholarship for the Grammar School I would say I quite enjoyed my schooldays. It is a funny thing, however, but if you won a scholarship in a community like that you became ostracized somehow and the last few months before I left were not so happy, although my main friends still remained the same. I had homework all through the week of course, but we would meet up at the weekends. I was the only one to pass the scholarship and the others just stayed on at school until they left at fourteen. Some of them went to work as shop assistants in, for example, the local drapers' shops, and in Thornbury, where their parents had to pay for them to be apprenticed. I think a couple of parents paid for their children to go to a school in Bristol where they learned commercial subjects.

Village life in the thirties varied on the size of the village and how close you were to the town. We had reasonable access to Bristol but it did cost money on the bus. Most of us therefore found our pleasure locally. We cycled everywhere, to distant villages and towns, and often a party of us would book a tennis court and have fun like that. There was a local cinema at Thornbury. This was wonderful and we probably went there about twice a week if we could manage it, but usually it was only to a Saturday afternoon matinee. That was quite a nice family affair as people took children and it was decent and the films were good fun. There were some very good films too. The actual cinema owner was a very far-sighted man. He and his brother did a lot in Thornbury. One started the gas works and this one opened the first cinema. As he was high on the film circulation list, being one of the earlier proprietors or owners, we often saw films at Thornbury before they were shown in Bristol.

There was also a large timber yard and it was common during the thirties and even early forties to see large timber wagons with trunks of trees on them, pulled along by a team of horses. I remember my mother used to take my little sister on her bicycle, sitting on the back in a little chair. She was coming up the hill from Thornbury once and one of these wagons got out of control. The horses bolted and this procession came down the hill at full speed zig-zagging across the road with the long trailer behind loaded with tree trunks. My mother was absolutely petrified and all she could do was to stand still and hope that when it reached her it would veer in the other direction. This yard is closed now and houses are built there. I may have confused you earlier when I said I was an only child and have now mentioned my little sister. As a matter of fact she wasn't born until 1940 during the bombing of Bristol. My mother, having had no children since I was born in 1922, had to go into hospital because of her age. She was forty. She was in hospital when it was bombed. It was very frightening for us at home, waiting and wondering.

I remember when I was a little girl seeing the aurora borealis or the northern lights as my father called them. Of course, in the country there were no street lights and we were used to walking looking at the stars, seeing which position they were in. My father could tell me about the Plough and other different ones. I remember also walking along one night and on the grass verge there were 'glow-worms'. My father picked them up and put them round the edge of his hat. I was thrilled as a little child seeing this. It wasn't until we moved to Thornbury, when I was thirty-two, that I ever had street lights. You get used to walking in the dark. You can see so clearly except when it is a really black night. There is nothing lovelier than the moon with the clouds scudding across the sky in a high wind.

In addition to the baker and the butcher visiting the villages we always had our groceries delivered. Usually a man from the grocery shop in the next village would come for the order and it would be delivered the next day. This went on even after the war for quite a long time. A couple of the shops in Thornbury had a mobile shop which would go round to villages. This was really a big lorry converted into a shop and was a great help for people especially in the days of petrol rationing and austerity. We also had what we called the 'Oil Man'. He had a huge lorry and it was literally decorated inside and out with all the things you could want in the way of saucepans and kettles, all the different appliances you would get in a hardware shop and, of course, he carried paraffin as most people had oil lamps, certainly up to the mid-thirties, even at Oldown.

One of the great events when I was a little girl living at Littleton was the local flower show, held in a village about 5 miles away. This was the big event of the year and there was a huge marquee with all the produce and then, of course, another one with cakes and sponges and home-made wines. Then there was the fun-fair and, as you can imagine, living in a very quiet little country village we thought it was marvellous to go out at night and see all the different roundabouts and things lit up and to hear the music. In fact, up to recent years we had a similar event in Thornbury but this has now been changed and we hold the flower show in a hall and there is a carnival in the daytime, but the magic has gone.

Of course, in the twenties and thirties people were very, very lucky if they could have a holiday. Not many people had paid holidays with their jobs. In fact I don't think any of the ordinary working people did until well after the war. I remember when my father started paying into a holiday fund from his work and that was not so many years ago. We did have one outing from the village and that was a Sunday school treat to Weston-super-Mare. The very earliest I can remember is going in one of the very old charabancs, if you can imagine them, with a large canvas top which was rolled back. This was when I was quite small, of course. Usually when we got to Weston the wind would blow and the sand would get into everything and we would all come home sunburnt, but having thoroughly enjoyed ourselves. The only advantage I had was that we had some of my father's cousins living at Barry, South Wales, and I was lucky enough to be able to go down and stay with them occasionally when my parents could afford the railway fare. That was very really nice for me. We couldn't go as a family but my parents managed to get me away for a few weeks in the summer. My cousins were, of course, town girls and they would take me around down to Barry Island and the different places of interest. I didn't like the noise there so much.

When we lived at Littleton we had a rector and I remember my father saying that if we didn't go to church on a Sunday he would be at the house the next day asking why. This rector said rector meant ruler! When we moved to Oldown my father said he was having no more of this and we went to church as and when we felt we wanted to go. However, I had quite a thorough grounding in religion, and it was not a strict family home. It was a happy home and, although my parents were young, they were brought up to live decently and there was no swearing in the house although we heard plenty of it in the village. The farm workers in particular weren't choosy in what they said. One just took it for granted but my father wouldn't have it in the house.

I remember at Littleton when I went to see my grandmother, having to cross over ditches with little bridges made of tree trunks cut in half and these could be very slippery. I remember falling off one into the ditch below and hurting my arm and also my eye. I had to go into Almtree Hospital for a few days for treatment on my eye.

Then in 1939 the war came, and life changed completely for us. It was still a village but the girls were required to undertake war work and some volunteered. A friend of mine was in the Land Army but she wasn't stationed locally, she was up in Moreton-in-the-Marsh. Another friend was in the ATS and later, after the war, she died from the effects of gun blasts. She was on an ack-ack station and the gun blasts ruined her lungs. A lot of us lost touch after we left school.

During the war everyone 'Grew for Victory' as they called it and we had plenty of vegetables, even though meat and butter and things like that were in short supply. My mother always managed to feed us reasonably well. We had meatless days and the days when swede and turnip were shoved into a pie instead of meat were terrible.

CHAPTER SEVEN

BIRMINGHAM MEMORIES

I have included this chapter on childhood in the city in order to bring out the differences and similarities between town and country life. There were far fewer differences in the style of life of the poorer people than might have been imagined. People were just as restricted to the areas in which they lived and worked and attitudes within the family were much the same in the city as in the country. Mrs Valente was born on 25 November 1919 in the parish of Deritend, near the city centre of Birmingham, in the district of Balsall Heath.

I had an older brother and sister. I came from a background of working-class people and we lived in a small back-to-back house in a long street of the same type of house, with a courtyard at the back with more of the same houses. So you see we lived in very congested conditions.

In the courtyard at the back there was also one brew house, a small brick building which housed a large brick boiler under which a fire had to be lit to heat the water. The only water tap was in this brew house. So all the water for each family's needs had to be fetched in some sort of container. The toilets were also in the yard. Two families shared one toilet, which had a lock, and those two families had to keep that toilet clean.

Even though we were poor people, living in seemingly poor conditions and in sparsely furnished houses, everything was always kept clean. There would be home-made cloth rugs on the floors. The house was lit by a lamp in the living-room which had an open fire grate on which all the cooking was done and food was never so good as the cakes and meats cooked in those ovens.

By mutual consent the brew house was used by each family one day a week for all their family washing. They would be responsible for lighting the fire underneath the boiler with wood and coal slack (coal dust) because this would burn slowly and was very cheap to buy.

On our day my sister and brother would light the fire to get the water good and hot, ready for our mother when she came home from work and she would often be in the brew house till quite late at night, washing by candle-light.

My mother worked hard in a factory because this was the early 1920s and life was very hard. England was still struggling in the aftermath of the First World War.

Unfortunately, like a lot of men in those days, my father was under the influence of the demon drink and even though I look back on my childhood as a happy time, I realize that my father's drinking habits caused a lot of tension in our life, and always did. It is only now that I am aware of how hard not only my mother, but women generally had to work in those days to keep their family fed and clothed as decently as their small income would allow.

When my sister and brother went to school, before I was old enough to go, they would take me to our grandma's, who lived a few streets away. They would leave me there while they were at school. The school was in Grandma's street, so they would also come and have their dinner at Grandma's and then go back for the afternoon session. At 4.30 p.m., they would fetch me from Grandma's and take me home, then would probably have a little chore to do for our mother before she came home.

I liked staying with our grandma. She was very good to us even though she herself had always worked very hard. My mother was the youngest of the sixteen children she had had although she had lost at least four of them at birth. As my mother was her youngest child I only ever knew about four uncles and one aunt; my sister remembers more of them but she is over seven years older than me.

Grandma would tell me about her life. She, again, had had a very hard life and she told me how my grandfather (Mother's father) had been a master slater and would have to go for work away from home and she wouldn't see him for weeks. She would be without money and she and the youngest of her children would have to go into the workhouse at times. Then he would come home with a bit of money, stay a while and then go away again leaving Grandma, often as not, expecting another baby (my mother would tell me in later years). I am glad I wasn't a wife or mother in those days, but even then, if a neighbour was in trouble all the other neighbours would rally round and help them, if they could.

When I was a child I had asthma and quite often I had to go to a hospital-like place in Steelhouse Lane called the People's Dispensary, because in those days visits to a doctor had to be paid for and the dispensary was free to poor people. I didn't mind going there. There were always lots of people and children there and I used to have medicine and large jars of cod liver oil and malt. I must have taken pounds of the stuff but it wasn't unpleasant, rather like thick treacle.

I was very fortunate though as we later left the city and went to Northfield to live among green fields and fresher air. This was when I was fourteen. My asthma got better and apart from odd times when I have been chesty, thank goodness I don't suffer from asthma now.

In later years my mother often said it was probably the cats that Grandma used to have to keep the mice down that caused it. That is why, I think, that while I am not afraid of insects, I am terrified of mice and rats, and also why I never have a cat or other animal at home.

We were fortunate in a way because we didn't get rickets like a lot of children did in those days. Mother and Gran would see that we had good wholesome, if plain, food.

I do not want to dwell too much about how we were always thought of as poor children, because our parents always tried to do their best for us. We didn't have all the sophisticated toys that children have today. Most of our games were street games anyhow. Because there was no traffic on the streets then, this was no problem. We would play hopscotch with a small piece of wood or large flat stone and a piece of chalk. We would have a long piece of rope for skipping, which we would beg off a local greengrocer. The fruit in those days was either in barrels or boxes, tied up with sisal ropes and it was these that the greengrocer would give us.

We used to devise a lot of our own games. I remember we used to cut out pictures from papers or comics (there were none of the nice magazines like there are today). We would put these pictures between the pages of a book and then we did a strange thing, of which I've never been able to find out the origin. Our playmates would bring a pin, a straight one, and put it between the pages and then whatever picture was in that page, they could have it and we kept the pins and gave them to our mothers. I've often thought about this since and I think that perhaps it was because pins were either in short supply or were expensive to buy. We used to call this game Pin a Pick. There were lots of games we would play outdoors, like hide and seek, which has been played by children for generations. We used to particularly like our game of hide and seek because the courtyards of houses I have told you about quite often led from one courtyard to another, so you can imagine it was very good to have so many hiding places, and to be able to fox the seeker.

Living in Grandma's house with her was my Uncle Tom, who had been very badly wounded in the war. He had been in the hospital for a long time because his wounds wouldn't heal, they were shrapnel wounds. Either my mother or grandma would visit him often. He was in Highbury Hall, the Chamberlain home, which they had allowed to be used for a hospital for the wounded soldiers. We would walk to Moseley from Balsall Heath, it wasn't very far. When he came out of hospital he used to make brooches at home. I think it was by way of rehabilitating the men after the horrors of war. We used to sit round the table and help him to do this. We used to thread small coloured beads on wire and make butterflies and flowers. They were very pretty and then they were fitted with a pin on the back. I never knew what was done with them. Uncle used to have to visit the hospital and take these brooches back; perhaps they were sold for some fund or other at the hospital.

We used to go to the Baptist chapel opposite Grandma's house and some Sundays we would go three times a day. We liked to go and were encouraged to do so by our parents. On every annual anniversary my mother would always see that my sister and myself had a white dress and a wide ribbon sash, white shoes and ribbons for our hair, and a small posy to carry. We were excited the days before the actual event. Grandma, Mum and our cousin, Doris, would come to watch and it was a lovely day. At other times we would go to the Salvation Army Hall, a few streets away, and we used to enjoy that, singing all the catchy hymns. At Christmas the Army band would play on the corners of the streets and we would stand and sing with them.

These were such simple pleasures, but how we enjoyed them and how I wish we had photographs from these events, but we had no such thing as a camera. If you were lucky you might have been taken to a studio as my brother and sister were. I remember seeing a picture of them together. I think I was born when it was taken but I've never seen one of me. I'm almost sure the first picture ever taken of me was at my sister's wedding. I was about fourteen-and-a-half and was a bridesmaid. I remember we all went to a studio in Gooch Street over a shop to have the wedding photograph taken.

We never went on holidays, but most of our holidays from school were spent in one of our two local parks, Calthorpe or Cannon Hill. We mostly went to Cannon Hill, where there was a pond. We liked to fish in the pond with a net and a jam jar with a string handle. Our mother would make a bottle of tea and jam sandwiches before she went to work, for us to take for a picnic and we spent nearly all day there.

About once or twice a year we would go to a well-known beauty spot much frequented by us city people, the Lickey Hills at Rednal, and there were always long queues for the trams at holiday time. We loved it there, after all it was the only place then that was country-like for us. I don't remember ever going anywhere outside of Birmingham, but that wasn't so strange as in those times there weren't many cars. I can't remember knowing anyone who owned a car.

Then again, once a year, because we came under the heading of the poor children of the city, we would go on an outing sponsored by the Cadbury family, to their Manor Park. That was a lovely day. We would go on the tram from Balsall Heath, get off at Hole Lane and then walk up to Manor Park. We would go into the long hut made of logs and have tea. We would all be given a bag containing a small cake and sandwiches and a piece of fruit, and a cup of tea was also served to us. We would then play organized games in the park and have races with a small prize for the winners. This was another outing we enjoyed very much and would look forward to.

Every year our father would take us to the Onion Fair. This was an annual fair which was held in Birmingham at the Serpentine Ground in Aston. It was the biggest I have ever seen with roundabouts, swings, stalls and side-shows, etc. We would walk all the way from our house, there and back, and it would be quite late sometimes when we would be walking home. I would be so tired that Dad would carry me home on his shoulders.

Also living in Grandma's house was our cousin, Doris, whose parents had died. There were four children left orphaned, and various members of the family had taken them in to be one of their family. When you think that they would be having a struggle to feed their own children, it was a wonderful thing to do. Doris was the eldest of these four children so she came to live with Grandma, her father was one of Gran's sons. She was older than us and would often treat us to the pictures and buy us sweets because she went to work and had pocket-money.

Birmingham Memories

I haven't told you about my father. He was a silver polisher in the jewellery quarter of Birmingham, although he didn't actually do jewellery. His company, W.J. Myatt, were silversmiths and made presentation bowls and cups, silverware, tea-sets, etc. In fact there may be still some of my father's work in the Council House in Birmingham. He often mentioned he had polished certain things to be presented to VIPs and I know there was a candelabra in Marl Hall, Llandudno, Wales, a Birmingham Hospital Saturday Fund Convalescent Home which my father had worked on. I saw it myself when I went there when I was eighteen after an accident at work.

I often went to the factory where my father worked and it is still there now in Frederick Street, but no longer called Myatt's, of course. How I came to know it so well was because of my father's drinking habits. We nearly always had to go and meet him on Friday evenings when he came out from work, so that he wouldn't go into the pubs and spend most of his wages on drink. We weren't the only ones there; there were other wives and children waiting for the same reason. I think it was because of the dirty and dusty jobs they did that they would drink a lot, but I also know in my father's case that he had gone through the war as a very young man, which had left a great impression on him. Every time he was drunk, he would re-live what he had lived through and the horrors he had seen. Perhaps this was the reason lots of the men became drunkards and obviously they would be unaware and oblivious of what the tension of having a father who drank could do to his family. However, I loved him for all that because when he hadn't been drinking he was a different man.

When I was about five years old we left our house and went to live with Grandma because she had injured one of her ankles sometime before and was now quite lame. Gran's house was much the same as ours, but it did have a front room and an extra bedroom. Also there were only four houses in her yard so it wasn't quite so badly congested and it was nice having a front room, with a door on to the street. Our sleeping arrangements weren't so good. My brother shared a room with our uncle, our cousin shared Gran's room and my sister and I shared our parents' room. Fortunately it was a big attic room, right at the top of the house with a smaller area at the side, just big enough for a double bed which my sister and I shared.

We all loved being with our grandma. It was probably a bit harder for my mother, although I think she was happy there with Grandma as they were very close. There were more people for Mother to wash for but Gran would cook all the meals and she used to cook lovely stews and make bread puddings, all on an open fire grate with ovens.

I think it eased the tension with Dad a little. He would push Gran when she had to have a wheelchair to get about. My gran had been widowed for many years. We never knew our grandfather so Gran had always had a struggle because Uncle Tom was never really able to do a proper job and I don't know what pay he had, if any. I know my grandma only had 10s a week because we used to have to fetch her pension from the post office.

Another everyday feature of life in those days were the pawn shops. You would see queues of women waiting with bundles, containing the family wash, or if their husbands owned a suit, that would go too. Looking back, even though I did go with my mother at times, I can't imagine what they would have in the bundles because none of them had very much. I think, if I remember rightly, it would be mostly pillowcases, bed-linen, tablecloths, etc, that is if they had one of the latter. I remember our table in Gran's living-room was a wooden table which was scrubbed every day. Come to think of it, most of the floors in Gran's house were bare boards but the front room, which I can still see in my mind, was the best. It had red lino on the floor and a sofa with two armchairs, lace curtains at the window and a small chiffonier (the dictionary definition is a low movable cupboard with a top suitable for a sideboard and that's exactly what it was). It had two stuffed birds in glass cases on it. We were never allowed to play in the front room, but we would be allowed to lie on the sofa with Gran's shawl around us if ever we were poorly. It was used quite a lot at Christmas and we would decorate it with paper-chains and, as we never had a Christmas tree, we would get a wooden hoop from the greengrocer which came off the barrels that the fruit came in and we would bind it with coloured paper and tinsel and hang a few baubles on it. The front room had a small fire grate in it and it would look so cosy when the fire was lit.

We always loved Christmas, although we didn't have much. We never had poultry, we had perhaps pork or rabbit roasted. Mother would go to Colmans the butchers quite late on any Saturday evening or Christmas Eve as she could get whatever she wanted much cheaper then. My father always took us to the Bull Ring, about fifteen minutes walk from our house, and we would buy chestnuts and apples and oranges, again quite cheaply, off carts which had kerosene lamps hanging from them. Even now I can still bring the smells and sights to mind and remember how exciting it was, the Bull Ring on Christmas Eve.

Then we would walk home and have our bath in front of a big fire in a large shallow wooden tub which was used for rinsing the clothes on wash-day (it was called a 'swill tub'), then we would go to bed and hang either one of Mum's or Gran's stockings up. Next morning we would perhaps have a book and game or toy sweet-shop, only simple things. Once I had a rag doll Grandma had made. We would also have a few new pennies, an apple and orange and a few sweets. As I've said our parents always gave us as much as they could within their means.

When I was nine, we left our grandma's and came to live in Northfield. We were very sad to leave Gran's but we were growing up and my sister Rose was working by then so we were given a house on one of about four new housing estates the council had built to house families in a slum clearance scheme (how I hate those words). Our house was called a 'parlour type', for obvious reasons, and was on Merritts Brook Lane. As there were boys and girls in our family we needed three bedrooms. I must say that although at the time I hated leaving Gran, it was a nice house. We had a parlour living-room with a big Triplex cooking fire and grate, a kitchen with running water and a sink and cupboards, a boiler for the washing, shelves on which to put the cooking utensils and, because it had gas and electricity, Mum and Dad bought a gas cooker. It was black, but a luxury, never mind the colour! Three bedrooms and a bathroom with a wash-basin, bath and toilet. You can imagine it was like going into a palace. We also had a large garden at the back and a fenced-in front garden and we were only 1½ miles or so from the Lickeys (the countryside).

The new house was going to be a struggle as it was a lot more rent than Mum had ever paid and we only had the bare necessities. In fact, it was ages before the front room was even furnished. So life went on. All the family but me would go back to the city to work. I remember the first day that I was really going to be alone in our new house. Mother had been at home a few days to get the house ship-shape. I hated the thought of being alone, but because there was no school, as yet, for us children who had moved from the city, I would have to stay alone while everyone was at work. I wanted to go back to my old school but that wasn't possible so, because I got upset, my mother took me to Grandma's.

I can't remember quite how long it was before schools were found for us, but at last we were allocated schools in the surrounding districts of Cotteridge and Kings Norton and then Northfield Village School also took in a few of the younger children. I went to Kings Norton, near the Green, where I was happy but then I always liked being at school. My husband-to-be, Dennis, moved from the city the same time as we did. I didn't know him then though. We were to meet later at Tinkers Farm School. He went to St Joseph's RC School. We had to travel to these schools by charabanc provided by the education department and we were picked up at three different points on the estate. We had to take a packed lunch and the school gave us a hot or cold drink.

Finally, in 1931, the site for Tinkers Farm School was obtained and we were housed in huts around the perimeter of the site until the school we had watched being built was finished and then we moved in to the new school in 1933. I left in 1934, only attending the new school for just over twelve months. I sat for what was then the secondary school exam at Kings Norton Girls (they were called grammar schools then). I passed but before the results went out my mother had a baby on 9 August 1932. She had given up work earlier in the year and I was overjoyed about Tony. I loved him but unfortunately I was never able to go to Kings Norton Girls' School. My mother told me I wouldn't be able to go and Miss Shepherd, my teacher, even came to our house to see if it wasn't possible some way. My mum had to tell her she couldn't possibly manage to buy books, uniform and everything I would need. I think my mother was always sorry about this but I understood; we had a new baby to feed and my mother had always had to struggle. She was still in bed after having Tony a few days before and she wasn't well. When Tony was eleven months old I came home from school to find my mother in a state of collapse and she was rushed in to Selly Oak Hospital. She had a diseased kidney which had to be removed and she was quite ill for a long time, so I had to look after Tony. I was allowed to go to school later but I had to take Tony, plus all his baby needs, to an older cousin who had moved onto the estate and she looked after him while I was at school.

My mother recovered and, shortly after, my sister left home and went to live with Gran again, so we had to move to a smaller house. I left school in 1934 and started to work at a small dressmaking firm as a general dogsbody at first. I sewed on buttons and hooks and pressed dresses and delivered them in boxes; dresses were packed in boxes in those days. I carried six boxes in each hand, they weren't heavy, and delivered to most of the wholesalers in the city. These wholesalers have vanished now but they were dotted around the Old Square area, Cherry Street and Deritend, so it is no wonder I know the city so well.

I was able to get the chance to better myself a little after not being able to go to secondary school. The small firm I worked for in Hinckley Street, at the back of the old Rep Theatre, was called The Beau-Monde and was owned by a Mrs Myatt, the same name as the firm my father worked for but I never found out if she was one of that same family.

One day, during the lunch hour, I had come up to the pressing room from the basement where we could make tea and eat our lunch. It was a bit grotty but it was only a small concern with forty people on the payroll. I heard the phone ringing in the office and it kept ringing and ringing and though I don't think I had ever spoken on the phone before, without thinking, I picked up the receiver and said 'Hello'. It was Mrs Myatt. I remember being so frightened I could hardly speak but she asked for one of two girls in the office, but they had gone out. When Mrs Myatt sent for me to come and see her in the office, I thought I was going to be told off and sacked. I thought my dad would kill me if I lost my job. She asked me how I'd come to be in the office and I said I wasn't. I had just come from the basement and because the phone didn't stop ringing I thought I had better answer it. She asked me how I would have answered it if it had been someone wanting to make an order, so I said I would have written everything down and given it to Miss Chatterley. She then gave me a job in the office and paid for me to go to the Chamber of Commerce in New Street to learn shorthand and typing.

My father's drinking habits never altered and sadly he passed away at the age of forty-five, when I was twenty-one. He had lost his job at Myatts through losing time at work, most Mondays after his weekend drinking bouts. He then worked at the Austin Factory in Longbridge until 1941 when he died. What a waste!

I have found it very hard to try to convey the fact that we were a typical family of those times. I know families who did live and come from the same background as I did and I am sure they would all agree with the saying 'Ignorance is Bliss' and that we didn't think that we were poor people then because we were all the same. We had no one to compare ourselves with. We got so much pleasure out of the simple things of life then. Now, even though we have our televisions and radios I don't think we really get any more pleasure out of them. We may not have to work so hard as the women of the 1920s and '30s, but the pace was much slower then.

Not only did my mother and gran work hard, but my sister, our cousin and myself did too. My grandma's house had to be scrubbed from top to bottom each week, she insisted on that and we had to help. The only place we had in which to wash our hands and face was a bowl on a broken, backless chair in a small larder off the living-room or in the brew house when it was warmer. When I tell you that there wasn't any furniture in any of the bedrooms but the bed and perhaps a broken chair, you will appreciate the conditions in which most of us lived. The adults would go to the public baths for their baths.

I hope I have been able to give you some idea of what it was like in those days, but really I've only scratched the surface. I used to come home from school when all the family was at work, in those days in Merritts Brook, and I used to have to clean out the fire and re-light it and start on the dinner. When my mother was in hospital I had to do everything for Tony, bathe him, keep him clean, and because babies didn't seem to be weaned so early in those days, I used to prepare all his feeds to take to our cousin's each morning. I had to do all the things for Dad and my older brother as well – washing, ironing and so on. Perhaps after all I did experience very early in life what a woman's role in the house was in the thirties.

The author helping Grandfather in the harvest field, 1929 (Author's collection)

Summer holidays on the beach (Author's collection)

The maypole, c. 1930 (Poole)

The boys' brigade on parade, c. 1930 (Oborne)

Playing in the stream, c. 1920 (Wright)

Riding home, c. 1930 (Fleming)

West Hatton Junior Scholl, 1920 (Parrott)

A game of tug of war, from a postcard, c. 1910

Bath night, c. 1910 (Author's collection)

At the cottage door, c. 1910

A popular pastime, from a postcard, c. 1910

The Sunday school outing, c. 1910 (Parrott)

A young farmer with his chickens (L. Powers)

Playing in the barn, c. 1930 (Longhurst)

Young anglers, 1930 (Author's collection)

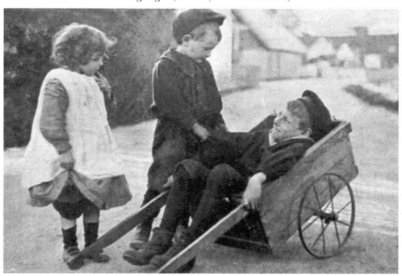

The lazy horse, c. 1910 (Author's collection)

Games on the village green, c. 1910 (Author's collection)

WAITING FOR FATHER.

The farmer's daughters, c. 1910 (Author's collection)

Posing for the photographer, c. 1910 (Author's collection)

CHAPTER EIGHT

A WILTSHIRE BOYHOOD

From Wiltshire we have the story of Mr Rupert Cove, who was born on
2 August 1920 at Gaskells Farm, Winstone.

My mother came from a little village the other side of Devizes
called Urchfont where her father was a small farmer. My father
came from Brokenborough, near Malmesbury, and his parents were
also farmers. My father took the tenancy of Gaskells Farm when he
came here. I attended Winstone C. of E. School and I spent my
whole school life there. The pupils at the school ranged from the
age of five years to fourteen and when I attended there were sixty-
five children at the school. We had three teachers, including the
head teacher. They were all lady teachers and they kept us in good
order. I left school when I was fourteen years of age.

We boys played cricket and football and when we were smaller
we used to play rounders. My father farmed the little field in front
of the school and he used to let us go out there whenever we
wished, evenings and school breaks.

There was no running water at the school and we used to have
to take a bucket out of the school and dip it down the well, which
was about 50 yd away from the school. Many a time when it was
our turn, the bigger boys used to throw the bucket in instead of
dipping it, then we had to retrieve it by going up to Mrs Haywards
and getting three hooks on a piece of rope and that used to take a
long time. This was one way of avoiding lessons. As regards hot
water, there were two fires in Winstone School and if you wanted

any hot water you had to fill a big kettle and stand it on the top of the fire.

For lighting we had two oil lamps which hung from the ceiling, there was no electricity. There still isn't any street lighting in the village. Many children had some miles to walk to school. One family, called the Partridges, had to walk from what was called the 'Villas' which is the other side of the main road. This entailed a walk of 3 miles. One of the lads from this family had a prize as he never missed one day's school for twelve months. They walked in all weathers, wind and rain, and they were never late, him and his sisters. They would come to school some mornings drenched to the skin. There was a fireplace in the school which had a very big high guard around it and the teacher used to hang their coats, and I can remember seeing their boots, round the fireplace. In those days there were no wellingtons. None of the children were collected from school even when it was dark. Usually we came out of school at 3.30 p.m. but in the winter time we finished at 2.45 p.m.

In those days there were no school dinners. Some of the children used to bring sandwiches but those of us who lived in the village used to go home. There were about thirty houses in the village and these were all stone built cottages. Everyone had to fetch the water for washing and cooking from the well and carry it home. We only had one well in the village which served everyone and for those who lived at the edge of the village this often meant a walk of half a mile, which was hard work. Sometimes the ladies fetched the water, but more often than not it was the men. Our carter, who lived at Gaskells Farm, used to fetch two buckets of water on a pair of yokes. He always had a cross made out of two sticks to stop the water from slopping. You just put the two bits of wood across the pail and that stopped it slopping out.

Wash-day at home was always on a Monday. Mother used to light the copper up and have a big galvanized bath to do the actual washing in and then it all had to go in the copper. It was then hung on the line which was at the side of the house. My mother never had a mangle or a wringer or tumble drier or anything like that. The majority of houses had an outhouse where the washing was done. Our copper was in a shed we used to call the brew house, I don't know why it was called that but it was used as a wood shed and there was this big copper in the corner. Water was not laid on in the village until 1948 and electricity the following year.

When I was about eleven years of age I used to help milk the cows in the morning before going to school. After school I would go home and change into some old clothes and get the cows in and tie them up because they were all in single stalls round the yard, not like it is today. Then I would have a cup of tea and go and help the men do the milking again. In the root hoeing time, when Father and the men would have been hoeing all day, Father would say, 'Come on my boy, I want you to come with me tonight and horse-hoe them mangels back' and that was it. While my father was doing that you could look across to the field and see other boys playing cricket and that didn't go down too well.

I can remember when I first started milking in 1932 as that was the year my grandfather died. It was on a Sunday afternoon, and I was up in the top cowshed, as we called it, milking a cow called 'Gertie'. Both me and Gertie had a bit of a shock when I heard he had died.

In those days it used to be pretty rough in the country in the winter because the winters used to be a lot worse than they are now. We used to get heavy snow and it used to be level across the fields from wall to wall. We boys used to have a good time snowballing. There used to be a wall between some of the houses and the fields which ran right up our street. We could make a lot of snowballs and get the other side of the wall and throw them at people's doors. One day there was no snow about but somebody had tipped some old potatoes on the lane leading up to the village hall. A gang of us got some of the potatoes and went to attack some poor old gentleman's door. We used to pick on the old ones because we knew they couldn't run, and this man always sat indoors with his bowler hat on, repairing clocks. Instead of the potato hitting the door it went through the window and knocked his hat off. The next morning we had the village policeman at the school.

The policeman did not live in the village but came from Burdock, which was 4 miles up the Gloucester Road and he always had a black Labrador dog running beside his bicycle. If he happened to be coming down the Pike Lane during the summer nights when it was light and we happened to be not working, we used to scarper, so he never saw much of us.

The village hall was near the school but was seldom used except at Christmas. The lady who lived at a nearby park in those days always gave the children a party and a Christmas tree. We used to have the party down in the school and then go up to the village hall to have the presents, where the tree was.

We always wore short trousers to go to school. In fact, when it came time to wear long trousers we used to put them on when it was dark as we didn't want to be seen wearing long trousers till we were fifteen. I have recollections of a tailor calling at the school to measure both me and my brother for a suit of clothes which had short trousers. Mother used to have our feet measured to have our shoes made as she insisted on hand-made shoes.

We had a blacksmith in Winstone. His name was Mr Barrett and I still have a chisel and a punch that he put my name on about forty-five years ago. There wasn't a thing he couldn't do. He was a marvellous old man. He used to shoe all father's horses in his younger days and he used to make casement windows and he was one of the best in Gloucestershire, they used to say, for dressing tools for stone masonry, regards chisels, hammers, etc. The men used to come from miles around to see Mr Barrett, bringing their tools when they were partly worn. There was one family in the village which were practically all stone masons.

There were no shops in the village other than a sweet shop where you could go and buy a ha'penny worth of sweets. The grocers had people which we called 'outriders' in them days, they would call and take the order on a Tuesday, then the grocery would come the following Tuesday. They used to bring it round when I went to school with two horses and a wagon. The butcher used to come round sat up on his cart with the meat and our place generally used to be the last house on his list. By the time he got up to Gaskells Farm the meat van was empty. There was a fishmonger came later on but in my school-days there was no fishmonger whatsoever. The baker used to live up on the Gloucester Road. He used to deliver the bread round in a horse and trap and later he had a lad with a bike, who helped out.

It was a very rare event to go in to Cirencester. I can remember once mother buying a 'Blue Flame', an oil cooker made by Valor. Me and one of the men who worked on the farm went in the pony and tub to fetch it, which was a very big occasion. The tub was pulled by a pony called Gypsy. Poor old Gypsy not only pulled the tub about but if they wanted a spare horse on the farm, he had to go along with the others in the team and do a bit of rolling and harrowing. He was rather a big, oversized pony. The tub had a shape similar to a tub but when you went to get up into it you had to go up a step at the back through a door. There were several types of horse vehicles for transport in those days – the gig, the rallycar, and the float as well as the tub.

Our house was the only one in the village with indoor sanitation in the bathroom. It was put in, along with the well out by the back door, when Father moved in in 1920. They used to have to screw a bung in the pipe where the water came up through and that would drive it right through up to the top of the house. The tank held roughly 200 gallons and it used to take about three-quarters of an hour and you had to work hard to pump it up there. The pump was situated in the well, nearly down on top of the water. Perhaps once every two years the rubber got worn and the blacksmith used to come from Miserden and they would let him down into the well on a wagon rope. But he always dropped a candle down the well first on a piece of wire to see if there was any gases or anything which would make it unsafe for him to go down.

I can remember when I was at the farm with my uncle and we had been combining with some very damp wheat on the Saturday. On the Sunday we were not allowed to work, so on the Monday morning we went to start the drier up and it would not run out of the grain pit through the wall into the elevator. This meant someone had to go down into the pit to disturb it, so I started to go down the ladder into the pit where the elevator was situated. Then I started to lose the use of my legs and my body and I scrambled back up quick and sat on the top. My uncle asked what was the matter and I said I would go down steady next time. I went down a rung at a time; every rung I went down seemed to make my legs weaker and it was caused by the gases that had collected over the weekend from this damp wheat.

In my school-days we never mixed with the girls. We would never sit by a girl – if we had to it was very much against our will. With regards playing with girls, I can never remember doing so. Girls as far as we were concerned didn't exist.

We had one teacher, a Miss Croaker, she was a marvellous lady. She was ill for a long, long time though and we had a relief teacher come who was 'a proper old boiler'. We found the cane and it got broken and we hid it. Our real teacher, well it was a crime for her to use it. She was very kind but if we misbehaved she only had to put her finger up once and that was it, we knew what she meant. Her voice was enough and the look she gave us! Her and her mother used to live in the schoolhouse and we used to get up concerts and her mother used to make all the costumes. I can remember we used to have to go along to the house and dress up and we used to be able to get a stage from an old gentleman. Someone used to fetch this stage on a horse and wagon and erect it in Winstone School and we used to give concerts in aid of getting a new piano. A Mrs Wills topped the list with a gift of £50, which was an awful lot of money in those days. We couldn't rely on the education authorities getting one for us even though the old one was getting so bad that every time we moved it a leg fell off.

At the age of fourteen I was living at home with my parents. They were farmers so naturally enough I stayed at home on the farm when I left school and started work full time straight away. In those days everything was done by horses on the farm. Father loved horses and if anybody mentioned a tractor to him it was no good at all.

I didn't start going to plough until I was fourteen-and-a-half. My father had bought a little plough off a neighbour and said to me one day, 'Come on, you've got to start to go and plough'. I had already been working horses and I broke in a two-year-old colt named Jolly and we had a piebald mare, which was a marvellous old mare to work the furrow, so we set off that afternoon to go to plough.

All through the season there were sheep to help look after and when the roots wanted horse hoeing, you had to lead the horses for the other men to hold the hoe behind. When the harvesting time came you had to help load the wagons, which was the easiest job. In haymaking you were up on the rick with a fork to level the hay a bit and get the hang of the job.

My father would plant about 3 or 4 acres of mangels every year and they would have to be pulled and put in heaps and covered up with leaves when it was a nice dry day. The leaves kept them dry if it rained and stopped the frost getting at them. If you had a couple of hours' rain in the night you would have a morning's hauling and then if the sun came out, you went pulling again in the afternoon. The turnips and the swedes were pulled for the cows to eat after they had been ground up to be mixed with the chaff and the meal. The ladies in the village sometimes used to come and pull some of the roots at 1s a cartload. My job was to haul them from the field up to where the cows were, to be pulped up and you were always told to take the biggest cart, to move as many as you could at one time.

When I started work after I left school I earned 2s 6d a week and my keep. My brother and I had half a crown each. I was older than him, about fifteen months. Mother put two half-crowns on the chest of drawers every week and as time went on I was doing more work than him so I wanted more money. I got a rise to 3s. Mother did all the books, we never consulted Father at all. She was the boss from the money point of view. Mother used to cash a cheque every week with the outrider from Gilletts the grocers to pay the other chaps. I think their wages then were about 30s a week. At haymaking and harvest time when they did overtime Father used to give them £1 for haymaking and the same for harvest; they used to be well satisfied with that. All the men lived in cottages on the farm and they used to work weekends for the rent which was supposed to be 6s a week. They also had a pint of milk a day, sometimes it was a bit more but nothing was ever said.

In the village we had a Baptist chapel, a Church of England church and some years ago there was a little hut where the Plymouth Brethren gathered (referred to locally as Plymouth Rocks). The Plymouth Rocks used to meet on the Gloucester Road in their little tin hut and the man who used to get up on the box and spout was the village blacksmith. He was a very good speaker and he wouldn't do any work whatsoever on a Sunday, but if he mended a puncture for you on a Saturday and you happened to see him on the Sunday morning and offered him the sixpence, he would take it. You used to see him get his bike out and cycle up the road on a Sunday morning about quarter to eleven, and again in the evening. I suppose in them days he would get sometimes twenty people in the congregation. Some people would walk from Winstone across the fields to the chapel and in the summertime he would take us children to the outdoor meetings in other villages, where we would stand out on the street listening.

The Baptist chapel was next door to where the blacksmith lived and Mr Hardingham was the preacher there. He was a grand old gentleman. He used to walk up and down the hill every day from the post office, which he kept, to Gaskells Farm to fetch his pint of milk and never said a bad word to anyone. When I was a lad he bought a gramophone and we children thought it was great. He used to have us in the chapel to listen to the records but I cannot remember what they were about. There was also a caravan which the farmers used to move about with horses from village to village and that was called the Church Army and that man used to preach up in the chapel in the evenings. I think he used to stop in the village for a fortnight and they used to park the van in the field just at the front of the school.

The church was at the bottom of the village and in my school-days the vicar lived in the old rectory. The vicar was the Revd Archibald Trotter. He was getting on in years and another grand old man. He used to come up to the school on Friday mornings for scripture lessons, which used to get a bit boring for us children. I am certain sometimes we used to nearly doze off. When he retired we had Revd Mills who lived at Sutgrove and he used to travel back and forth in his little Singer motor car, which some of the boys thought was very attractive. In those days there was no car-park in front of the church; people used to have to park their cars at the end of the road. I never got tangled up with this bit of mischief but I know a certain number of the lads used to watch the vicar go into church and then get in the car and drive it up and down the road. Anyway, someone found out and warned them the policeman was going to come so they stopped that. They weren't satisfied, however, and after it had died down a bit they thought they would still have their bit of fun and they went along to the church one night when they were at service and jacked the car up with stones off the wall. When poor Mr Mills came out to go home, you could hear him because he was a bit heavy-booted on the throttle. He put his foot down and nothing happened – the back wheels just went round and round. Fortunately there was no damage done.

A little later I can remember I sometimes went to church with a mate of mine on Sunday nights, especially in the summer. I was old enough to go to pubs then, although when I wasn't old enough I still used to go, put it that way. As soon as the service was over we would walk out up the croft and Mr Mills would come up and say, 'Would you two boys like a lift? I know where you are going.' We used to say, 'Thank you very much sir', and get in. He used to take us to Missenden, pull up outside the pub and say, 'This is your destination'. Then he used to bid us good night.

When we were at school we used to play a game, 'Tap, Tap the Spider' we called it. We had a safety pin which had a piece of cotton threaded through the little loop with a button on the end. We stuck the safety pin into a window ledge, and could then pull the end of the cotton which made the button tap on the window. Mr Hardingham lived down in the post office which had a window looking across the road. On the other side of the road was a bank and a field in which we could get up out of sight. Anyway we used to get the button going and, of course, the poor old man used to wonder what was going on. We even used to make sure he couldn't get out of the other door by tying a piece of rope on the handle and putting a broomstick across the porch. This particular night we had it working well but we didn't realize he had somebody stopping with him. It was in the days when flashlights were becoming popular. All of a sudden the door opened and this light appeared and there was four of us doing it, me, my brother and two more lads. My brother and his mate ran off across the field but me and this other lad made up the field. There was a quarry there and we dived in to be out of sight and there were stinging nettles and, of course, we had short trousers on, which wasn't very comfortable. We had to sit it out till the man with the flashlight went back in but he never caught us anyway.

The man who used to come as Attendance Officer when I was at school was a Mr Burton and he was a right comedian. We used to be frightened to death of him. If we stayed away half a day, he would be knocking on the door threatening to lock our mother up or fine her or something or other. Anyway, he was followed by a more likeable sort of a man, Eddie Walters, who was still there when I left school. We didn't have much bother with him because we never had many days off from school. We used to be frightened to stay at home and we never used to run away hunting unless it was at dinner time, when we might be half-an-hour late coming back into school. Sometimes we used to get told off but I don't think we got in too much bother. The only time we used to get into a bit of a quandary at the school was when the men went back to work. They all worked on the farms, but they used to live down by the school you see. There was some snow on the ground once and we used to snowball them and, of course, they would snowball us back. This one particular day, I can remember, me and another lad, we were on the men's side. We got outside and somebody had opened the porch door where all the little kids' clothes were hung and the snow went all in the porch. Our schoolteacher made us go and clean it out and we had to go in to school, but that didn't bother us because we weren't having lessons.

The nurse who came to the school and looked through your hair was called the 'bug hunter'. She looked in your hair to see if you had any little nits and dobs flying about. When you pinched them with your two thumb nails you could hear them pop. I can remember our mothers used to do our hair with some type of disinfectant, because it was a crime in those days if the 'bug hunter' did find a nit in your hair.

I can still recall village life in my teen years. There were three of us and we used to ride our bikes from Winstone into Cirencester on a Saturday night. We used to get there about half past six, as far as I can remember, and park our bikes at the back of a man's shop for 2d. Then we'd go up to the Black Horse and have three half-pints of beer each, which was 3d per half a pint. Then we would go to the picture house, which was the Gaumont, which is no longer there, and that was 1s. We'd come out about half past nine and get our bikes and come back up Gloucester Street on the way home and have a plate of fish and chips for 6d and that was a great evening out. It used to take us half an hour to cycle each way to Cirencester, but we were young then. The main road was tarmacked in those days but the side roads were white stones.

The first bike I had was what mother bought us off one of the men who worked for us, for 5s. I was still at school then and it was put in a room and kept for us till we grew to the bike. This wasn't the cycle I used to ride to town though. I'd saved a bit of money by then and went to Cheltenham one Saturday night with uncle and bought a brand new Hercules bike for £4 19s 6d and that had cable brakes and a chain guard and if it rained I was reluctant to take it out.

We used to have dances down in our old village hut and occasionally they also ran a 6d hop to teach us to dance. I was one who couldn't learn. I was a bit pig-headed and used to sit out and watch the others, but now I wish I had. At Miserden, in the big house there was a lot of servant girls working and we used to congregate there and go and see the old landlord and his sister and have about a couple of half-pints. Then we would go along to the village hall, I think it was about 1s to go in.

Very often three or four of us would walk in the week from Winstone to Miserden just to have a drink and perhaps on a Saturday night we would get 'spoofins' for bars of chocolate, which in them days was 10d for half a pound. We used to enjoy this 'spoofin' lark which was when you all had some loose change in your pocket and you put your hand in and took out so many coins. You and your mates were all 'spoofin', so you put your hand out with the coins in it and everybody would try to guess how many coins there were. If you guessed the right number you were out and the last one go to out had to pay for all the rest to have bars of chocolate. We used to spend hours doing that. We used to do it at the old village pub at Winstone as well.

On the way home from Miserden the lads and the girls used to talk and we used to send some bars of chocolate up through the window on a piece of cotton. The girls used to drop the cotton down and we used to tie the bars of chocolate on for them. It would take us about half an hour to walk to Miserden. We never had no ale to carry but coming back it used to take a lot longer.

In my school-days a packet of crisps was 2*d* and one particular type was only 1*d* which were broken crisps. One of the landlords of the village pub was selling sweets and he had a ha'penny box — everything in it was a ½*d* Of course, us kids if we had 1*d*, we could come back with two lots, either a packet of sherbet or some sort of chocolate bar for ½*d* each. I can remember the sherbet in a yellow bag with a liquorice stick in the middle and you used to suck it out. There was another sweet-shop in the village owned by Granny Hayward.

Life in my young days was so different from now. There was no violence. The only time I can remember anything being pinched was when two lads came to school once. Grandfather had some sheep troughs up by the old Pound Cottage and they pinched a pair of grandfather's sheep trough wheels. The local policeman found out and they had to go to Cirencester. One lad had seven strokes and the other had eight with the birch. I sat at school with the one that had eight strokes and it was short trousers in those days and a couple of days later he said to me, 'I'll never pinch another thing, that hurt me'.

The village itself used to be centred around the church and the manor farm, but from excavations no trace of the original village can be found round there. The reason is possibly because with the coming of the Black Death all the houses were razed to the ground and there was just the church left standing.

CHAPTER NINE

TWO LINCOLNSHIRE LADS

Mr George Wilkinson and Mr Reg Mears sent us a taped record of their memories.

My name is George Wilkinson of Cissplatt Lane, Keelby, Grimsby. I was born on 1 April 1916. I am a retired farm worker. I have lived in a tied cottage all my working life. I have lived in Lincolnshire all my life. My mother and father lived in a tied cottage where I was born and Father was a shepherd. My father used to take sheep to the shows, the Lincolnshire and the Yorkshire. Several prizes were won with the Lincoln Long-wool sheep. I remember Dad telling me that one was sold for one thousand guineas. Lots of first prize winners were exported to the USA.

When I was eight years old Dad got tired of all the extra work in getting the sheep ready for the shows. We then moved to a farm 2½ miles away, where Dad worked again as a shepherd. After three years Mother and Dad went to Croxton and again he was a shepherd in a tied cottage. Dad looked after four hundred ewes but did not enter any for the shows. I used to go with him on Saturday mornings and helped to break the cake for the sheep. Sometimes the farmer would give me 6*d*. There were seven cottages on that farm and two more at the top yard. All the men worked on the farm, including the foreman and the man who looked after the fat beasts, cows and calves. There was another farm in Croxton as well, and there were six houses on that farm and seven or eight young people were of school age.

We walked a mile to school. We had a bottle of cold tea and a packet of sandwiches for our dinner. In May a maypole was fixed up in the playground and about five boys and girls used to dance round it each holding a ribbon, until the ribbon was wound tight then they went the other way round to unwind it. Someone played the violin for us to dance to.

We had no social life in the village apart from playing football. At home we had a wind up gramophone and a few records and we played it at night in the winter-time. When it was cold in the winter Mother used to put a brick in the oven until it was hot, then she would wrap it up and we would take it to bed to warm our feet. We had a paraffin lamp in the front room and candles to light us up to bed. There were only three fresh water taps in the village, the nearest one to us was about 100 yd away. We had a square wooden frame about 2½ ft square and we would fill two buckets with water and rested the frame on the top and then step in the frame and hold the bucket handles tight. In that way we could walk without the buckets knocking on our legs. Our next-door neighbour had a two-wheeled tank which held eight buckets and I used to borrow it to get water for wash-days, if it did not rain. I also fetched the water for next door as well for 3d a week.

Three of the cottages were what was known as 'cow cottages', they shared a small grass field half a mile away. In the summer one of the men got up at 5.30 a.m. and fetched the cows home to be milked. They used to milk their own cows and then go to work on the farm at 6.30 a.m. Their wives then put the milk through the separator and took the cream off. If the men worked overtime the women used to milk the cows. The cream was then put in a churn and turned by hand. The skimmed milk was then sold for ½d a pint. They also kept a pig and chickens. My father used to kill the pig for them just before Christmas. Each of the men had a cow stable at the top of the garden, which was about 35 yd from the house. The toilet was next to the cow-shed and there was a nice walk in the moonlight after tea. The lamp was used when it was dark.

One day when we were at school Lord Yarborough's foxhounds came past at the playtime, about 10.30 a.m. The meet was held at Pond Close Wood, half a mile from school. Three of my mates and me decided we would skip school and go to the meet, so away we went. We followed the hounds till 3.30 p.m. then went home, we had had no dinner. Mother wanted to know where our lunch bags were. We had left them at school. Next morning when we arrived at school the schoolmaster wanted to see us in his study. We all got several strokes of the cane. We did not tell our parents as we might have got into more trouble. Anyway, no more was said in that respect.

I left school at fourteen years old and was presented with a book inscribed 'G. Wilkinson. A Good Record' from the schoolmaster. I got on well with the school boss and he gave me a good written reference when I left. I then started work on the farm where we lived and my wage was 11s a week, from 6.30 a.m. to 5 p.m., and 1 p.m. on Saturdays. Another boy worked on the farm, he left school about the same time. One of the jobs we did in the summer was to cut the lawn twice a week. The lawn-mower was pulled by a pony, one of us leading the pony and the other steering the mower. We tied rubber boots on the pony's feet so it did not mark the grass.

When the corn crops were high enough we went with the man to cut the thistles. We each had a tool called a 'spittle', a long shaft with a T-shaped handle and a small blade about 2 in wide at the bottom. We pushed this blade under the thistles and cut it off below ground level. Later on the wheat, barley and oats were harrowed, then rolled. The harrowers and the roller were pulled by two horses. The harrows pulled the chickweed and some of the rubbish out of the corn and the roller brought the clods of soil up and crushed the stones in. Nothing more was done to it until the harvest time. Us two lads often got the job of rolling the corn.

In harvest time the corn was cut with the binder pulled by three horses. This machine tied corn up in bundles we call sheaves, and dropped them about 1 yd apart. The binder was driven by one of the horsemen. The labourers then went and picked up the sheaves and stooked them. That is they stuck them up something like a tent and put five sheaves each side. These stooks stayed in the field for two or three weeks to dry. The horses in the binder were only worked for two or three hours and then went home for a feed and a rest. Us two lads had the job of looking after the horses and changing them, one at the top yard and one at the bottom, when they had done their shift. The sheaves were then taken up to the yard in wagons and stacked. Then they were thatched with straw to keep the stack dry. When the stack of sheaves was high and out of the reach of the men emptying the wagons two stakes were driven in to the stack side and a board put on the stakes. One of us lads were then put on the boards and we had to take the sheaves from off the man on the wagon and hoist it up 6 ft or more to the man on the stack, using a two-tined fork, what we call a hay fork or pitchfork.

When the harvest was finished my mate and me then went to work in the turnip fields and later swede fields. We each had a two-tined fork about a foot long and a fairly heavy knife. We pulled the turnip up with the fork, trimmed the top off and cleaned the root by holding the knife in front and striking it with the fork. We could throw the turnip about 5 yd and make a heap. We would make a line of heaps about 10 yd apart, and put a wire fence in front to keep the sheep back. We then pulled a cut-box to each heap and one lad filled the cut-box while the other filled the sheep troughs with the cut turnips. They were like big potato chips. A man turned a handle to make the cutter work. Us two lads took the key-wedge out of the fly-wheel once and lost it. This meant that the cutter went in jerks making it very difficult for the man turning the handle. After about fifteen minutes or so to the great relief of the man, we found and replaced the key-wedge. The fields were very often 6 in deep in mud and the man carried the front of the box with two handles and we pushed behind. One day we had to go through a pit and

the man warned us to be very careful as it might tip over
sideways. Us two lads made up our minds when we got on the
pit side to push the cut-box over, which we did. The man was a
bit upset and one of us lads had to walk to the yard to get help to
get the cutter on its wheels and out of the pit. We had to give
the sheep extra cake that day as we lost one-and-a-half hours'
work cutting turnips.

We had a hut in the field where we had our lunch and dinner
and sheltered if it rained very heavy. The farmer supplied us
with a pail for a stove and we had to light the stove up about
7 o'clock in the morning for the breakfast at half past eight and
stoke it up again at 12.15 p.m. for our 1 p.m. dinner. We used to
try and get the hut very hot for dinner time and often the man
would go to sleep after dinner if we kept quiet so we often got
an extra ten or fifteen minutes for dinner. We went to work
from 8 till 12 on Sunday mornings on that job and we got 1s 3d
extra pay the first winter. The second winter our wages went up
to 13s a week.

When I was sixteen years old I told my boss I wanted to deal
with horses and earn more money. All his horsemen had signed on
for another year so I took on the job as second horseman at another
farm at Immingham. I stayed there three years.

*Mr Wilkinson introduced his friend Mr Reg Mears, a Lincolnshire folk-
singer. This is Mr Mears' account.*

In my school-days I can remember we were well looked after at
Brockerly Park School, at Limber Magna. A wonderful school it
was. Every pupil had a pair of slippers to put on when it was bad
weather as some as some of them walked miles to school. All the
little girls had a red cloak and they looked pretty on a winter's
day among the snow. After a while the boys had cloaks as well,
dark cloaks with a hood, but they soon wrecked those. They
didn't take care of them like the girls did. We were lucky really

as I don't think there was another school where they had cloaks and slippers. It was all due to the care of the Yarborough family; they supplied all these things for us at school. It was really wonderful.

I was always interested in wildlife from the very beginning and nobody told me about being a naturalist, I hardly knew what the word meant. I was crazy about wildlife, birds in particular. I had to catch them in an old parrot's cage, just to get them in my hand to look at them and then let them go again. I really loved these things and I still do. I used to climb up in the yew trees and wait for the birds to come near me so I could get a close look at them. As time went on I began to find out more about them and I learnt a lot from cigarette cards. I learnt to identify them and I got very good with getting all the song notes. That is the best way of identifying them if you know the bird songs, you cannot go wrong with that. You have to be careful as some birds can imitate others; an old starling can imitate anything. You think you are hearing something else when it is a starling. As time went on I met more people interested in birds. Earlier I accidentally got hold of White's *Natural History of Selborne* and as I read that I realized I was not as crazy as people thought I was. It boosted me up a lot. Now we have nature reserves, which is a great thing. If it weren't for nature reserves, goodness knows what the wildlife would do, it really is marvellous. You can go and see these things at the reserve and watch the birds contented.

There used to be hundreds of partridges when I was young but nowadays you only see a few here and there. Now I look after 1½ acres of woodland which I run as a kind of nature reserve. There is a good lot of oak in it. It had been let go and nobody had replanted it, so I took the worst lot of stems out and left the best ones to grow into good trees. We get a lot of warblers there, owing to a large amount of caterpillars. In the summer-time they breed and we have various breeds of warblers. I have left open spaces because warblers like open spaces where they can see what they are doing.

All my life, of course, has been spent at Limber Magna. I was born there, and the woods there have become my life. I don't believe in ghosts but if there is a ghost of me he will be walking about Limber Woods. I always had permission to go all over the woods and still do to study wildlife and enjoy the birds and it has been a great life.

In almost all the Lincolnshire villages, every year at the chapel there was what was known as the 'Anniversary'. On the Sunday, all the youngsters, the girls and boys, used to say recitations in the chapel and they looked very pretty. All the girls wore new dresses and they sang special songs. Then on the Monday we had what they called the 'School Feast'. We all gathered in the field in the afternoon and evening and there were two big swings beneath a great sycamore tree and there were plenty of volunteers to swing you beneath these trees and the lads used to swing the lasses. There was a coconut shy and then, at the end of the day, the last thing that happened was this kissing ring. We formed a great big ring, everybody joined in, old people, middle-aged and children, all the lot. There was one big ring on the outside, and inside that ring was a smaller ring. Some of the lads would go in that smaller ring and pick a girl out while we were singing this ditty:

> Oats and beans and barley grows,
> You or I or anyone knows,
> You or I or anyone knows,
> Where oats and beans and barley grows.
>
> First the farmer sows his seed,
> Then he stands, he takes his heed,
> He stamps his foot and he claps his hands,
> And turns around and views the land.

Waiting for a partner,
Waiting for a partner,
Open the ring and take one in,
Make haste and choose your partner.

Now you're married, you must obey,
You must be true, to all you say,
You must be kind and very good,
And help your wife to chop the wood.

Chop it thick and chop it thin,
Help your wife to carry it in,
When you leave give her a kiss,
And that's the way you all dismiss.

Oats and beans and barley grows,
You or I or anyone knows,
You or I or anyone knows,
Where oats and beans and barley grows.

When we got that one over, they would go back to the big ring and the girls would stay in the middle and pick a boy out while this ditty was being sung. This was how it was and everybody used to have a good time and it was a beautiful way of spending an evening all singing in the kissing ring.

CHAPTER TEN

HUNTINGDONSHIRE MEMORIES

Mrs Marjorie Jeanne Howard writes of life at Stanground, near Peterborough, and argues that 'times were hard but good manners came freely'.

I was born at 8 a.m. on Wednesday 29 August 1917 at Conygree Road, Stanground, Huntingdonshire, now Cambridgeshire, 3 miles from Peterborough. It was a quiet village with one church, one chapel, five public houses, two schools, a police station and a vicarage.

I started school aged five-and-a-half years, rather late, as I had measles then mumps and then had to wait until after the school holidays. Fortunately my father's sister was a teacher at a school where you had to pay 1*s* per week for tuition, so I didn't miss out. I rather think I benefited, as I was always ahead of the class, or so I was told. The school was an old building, with low tables and chairs, around thirty in a class. The one very big room had a glass and wood sliding partition to divide into two classrooms. The day always started with prayers and a hymn, as it was a Church school, the upkeep coming mainly from the Church. The vicar visited us at least twice a week for Scripture lessons. We were taught very thoroughly, with obedience and good manners being very prominent in our teachings. The girls were taught, even at this early age, to knit and sew. 'The Devil found work for idle hands' we were told over and over again. We had to make string dishclothes on large wooden needles, then seat covers for bicycles. These were sold at the church bazaars. I am still a keen knitter. When I look back the embroidery we did was very advanced for our ages. We did fancy edges to handkerchiefs first, then moved on to pillowcases and tablecloths. Eventually we learned drawn-thread work and smocking, for pinafores and little girls' dresses. This in time was a great asset to me as I had three daughters.

My parents were Florence Alice and Thomas Edgeley Howard. I was their first child, later having two sisters, but alas no brother. Father was a fireman on the LNER earning 22s (£1.10) per week. Mother had been living in service since the age of fourteen with her widowed grandmother, who kept an ale house and catered for boarders. The City Arms still stands in St Johns Street, Peterborough.

I can well remember sitting on the rag rug, in front of the shiny black-leaded fire grate, playing with the marble from a lemonade bottle, while Mother helped Granny with the endless cleaning. The fireplace had a boiler on one side with a shiny brass tap, their only means of constant hot water. The big dining-table was scrubbed white, then covered with a chenille cloth with bobbles round the edge when not in use. Mum used to push my sister in her pram the 3 miles each way and if I had been very good, I could have a ride on the way home, this before I started school of course. When I started school, we only went to Granny's on Saturdays.

My parents paid 3s (15p) per week for their first home. The house is still standing and today worth around £25,000. Six of the original terraced houses still stand after considerable renovations. The rest of the street has private retirement bungalows on that side and opposite, where Dad used to have an allotment to grow vegetables, is a residential home for the elderly and then more bungalows.

The Church school I first attended has been knocked down for property development, but the 'big school' in Chapel Street is still in use and is where my grandson started school. The thatched cottage and house-cum-post office has been pulled down to make way for modern houses but Vine House and other properties still remain. The occupant of Vine House was one of my first teachers, who died in 1988 aged ninety-nine years. The vicarage still stands, but alas, is now a bingo hall. In North Street two of the three pubs still stand. The property owned by my late grandparents, a bungalow standing in an acre of land, is now four bungalows each with a large garden.

I can remember when Grandma kept a village store there before the fire which gutted the thatched house, and the bungalow was built. She sold everything, including the vegetables and fruit which grew in the orchard all tended by Grandad. He never did any other work, except to light the village gas lamps, to the day he died aged seventy-six from a stroke after returning from that very task.

One Sunday when we were having tea there, a lady came to the back door asking for a teapot, as she had broken hers and had visitors. Grandma, who never refused a customer, realized she didn't have one but asked the lady to kindly wait while she went to the stock-room. To our amazement, she emptied the contents of our pot into a large jug, washed it up and wrapping it in brown paper, sold it for tuppence and we continued our Sunday as though nothing untoward had ever happened. Of course, we were never allowed to speak at the table anyway. Her actions showed great enterprise, and she died a wealthy and wise lady, and passed on to me much of her wisdom, I'm thankful to say. I can't imagine the nonchalant young shopkeepers of today ever doing such a kindness to oblige.

They were happy days in Stanground. We could play safely on the street pavements with whip and top, hoop-la, marbles and skipping, with no cars, buses or noisy motor bikes to mow us down, or fill our lungs with fumes. In Stanground now there is a rural bus service every thirty minutes on the roads where we used to play.

Everything was delivered by horse and cart. Milk came in large churns carried on a float drawn by a pony. Bread was carried in

huge, well-scrubbed baskets, which must have been heavy. All
bread was un-sliced and unwrapped but was really fresh daily and
the hot cross buns on Good Friday really were HOT, brought
around about 7.30 a.m. The errand boys rode cycles with huge iron
carriers, whistling happily as they delivered meat and groceries.
Everyone seemed so much happier then in the early 1920s, not
much money but plenty of love and care for everything and
everyone and neighbours were really neighbourly.

We went to church or Sunday school in our best clothes, twice
every Sunday. From spring to late autumn we visited the church
gardens at the vicarage, being told NOT to pick anything or trample
on the borders. We often saw the two tortoises and identified the
different birds with the vicar's wife and two daughters. It was lovely.
On Mothering Sunday we were allowed to pick and make our
mothers a posy of daffodils, muscaris and crocuses with evergreens.
Far better than the commercial way of today. Three little flowers to
represent the Holy Trinity woven with evergreens to denote ever-
loving. Everything was done with meaning and purpose in those
days. We valued the joys of nature, and were brought up not to take
them for granted. We were never allowed to walk on any cut grass
in the local park. We always played on the play grass, admiring the
flowers and appreciating their beauty. The park ranger in his
uniform carried a stick and, although I never saw him use it, I am
sure he had full authority and would have done so had the occasion
arisen. We respected him and what he stood for – law and order,
which preserved the park's beauty for everyone. In our days officers
of law and order, the police were seen everywhere and could give
any offender a 'good hiding' on the spot. Then when he or she
returned home, they got another one from father for bringing
disgrace to the family by being brought home by the village bobby.

On Sunday evenings in the summer, my dear grandparents took
my cousin Sydney and I for a ride in their pony and trap. This was
a lovely treat. We sat high up in the four-seater trap, on hard
wooden seats although we never noticed the bumps. Grandma had

a cushion and a rug to cover her knees, even when it wasn't chilly. She always wore black, I can never recall her ever wearing any other colour, though of course she was not in mourning – long black taffeta skirts which rustled as she moved, black high-buttoned boots and long gloves, topped by a black hat that had a veil over her face. She never removed it, even when being kissed in greeting by relatives.

Grandad sat up front holding aloft a whip, which he never used, clucking to Dobbin the dappled pony to 'Gee up'. We only travelled in daylight, but the trap had a lantern on either side, just in case. Trotting along the country roads, doing all of 3 miles per hour was heavenly when I look back. No loud transistors to drown the bird-song, no petrol fumes to mask the sweet smell of the lovely wild flowers, a pleasure to be alive in such good days.

The discipline of our youth stood us in good stead too. We dared not be late for school or it was the cane, boys and girls alike, no excuses. If you had an errand to run before school, as we often did, you started a few minutes earlier. It never did us any harm, I am a healthy active gardener in my seventies and hope to see the year 2000.

The strict discipline applied in the home too. We never left the table without asking if we could, then we sat quietly until the adults had finished. We always said, 'Thank you for having me' after attending a friend's birthday party, or after visiting relatives. The same common courtesy applied at Christmas. We spent all the morning on Boxing Day writing our 'thank you' notes to kind relatives, who had bought us a pencil and pad, or a ball of Rainbow wool and a pair of knitting needles, any small gift was acknowledged with thanks. After all, times were hard for most people in the early twenties and thirties, but good manners came freely.

When you next hear the clang of the fire-engine, imagine the wonderment, and even joy, of a child seeing six white horses, galloping along with firemen seated high on a tender full of water, their brass helmets and epaulettes gleaming, their black boots shining. One man would be sitting up front clanging away at a large brass bell and all the men would be shouting 'Fire' as the horses galloped along the streets. My great uncle was a fireman and I couldn't understand why he had a plaque with 'Fireman' over his door, yet my father, who was an engine fireman, did not.

Talking of shining boots reminds me how one Sunday morning when Grandma called to take me to church as usual, she asked if I had cleaned my boots. Although only seven years old at the time, I was taught to take them into the shed on Saturday and clean them ready to visit God's house next day. I made the excuse that I had been doing my piano practice until too late. 'Tut Tut', was the response from my grandma, who asked Grandad to attend to them, 'Please Thomas'. Oh my goodness! I had to go and sit in the Sunday school with one high-buttoned brown shiny boot and one white-washed one. This was to teach me to have self-respect and not to go about looking slovenly. One day after I had darned the hole in my stocking knee, it didn't look neat enough, so Mother cut a bigger hole round it and then made me darn it properly. Nothing was done in a shoddy way, 'either do it properly my girl or else'. It was wonderful training for after life of course, but we were not glued to the telly half the time then.

On Sunday evenings the families gathered in their homes and had a sing-song around the piano. It was lovely after a high tea, the aunts and uncles all contributing their party pieces. Don't get me wrong, I do enjoy the television, but when visitors come it is turned off. One cannot really make conversation with the ever-distracting square box butting in!

The churchyard lost its railings in the war years and is overgrown most of the time with weeds and litter now. The church still has two altar candlesticks, donated by my grandparents as a thanksgiving gift after their lives were saved when their thatched home caught fire in 1921. The huge oak candlesticks with brass holders came from their four-poster bed. I feel proud to this day when I see them. I was christened at that church and my parents and grandparents are all buried there. St John's church has a lot of memories for me; it was even in that churchyard that I received my first kiss from my future husband.

Clothing is another area which has changed dramatically. As girls we proudly wore our starched white pinafores, the broderie anglaise epaulettes and hand-knitted white lacy cotton socks with black patent shoes were nearly a Sunday uniform. Of course, it was long-buttoned boots and woollen stockings in winter. Boys looked nicer too, I recall my son wore short trousers at Stamford Public School until his fourteenth birthday, as part of his school uniform.

When I was nine-and-a-half I passed the scholarship and went to the Grammar School in Peterborough. I was so very proud and happy, as were all the family. Grandma gave me four half-crowns, now valued at 50p but wealth to a young girl. Of course, I had to buy my paints, crayons, pens and pencils with some of it and give 1s to the church as a thanksgiving but I still put 5s in my Post Office Savings' Bank.

My uniform was a brown tunic and oatmeal blouse, panama hat with band for summer, and a brown velour for winter. Our school motto was *Non Sibi Set Deo Et Alteri* – Not for oneself but for God and others. A very good motto I think. I still try to live up to it as much as possible.

At school I played hockey and tennis and was taught to swim in the outdoor pool for which the family had paid 25s to enable me to be a life member. Alas, the school has recently been taken over by property developers for flats for the elderly, costing around £35,000 each. I wonder if they ever hear the ghostly voices singing the school song sometimes. It grieves me to think the honours board was demolished, not preserved. I was proud of seeing my name on it with four honours gained or earned in my senior Oxford exams. My certificate was lost in the Blitz unfortunately. Still I can remember most of the things I learned and try to pass them on to my fifteen grandchildren and seven great-grandchildren. I hope they will be willing to learn. We were always urged and cajoled to do our best at school. One year I had come top of the form two terms in succession and because I was only second in the third term, I was asked what was wrong and why had I let someone beat me? Second out of forty-two isn't so bad, but of course it wasn't first and I had already proved that I could do that.

Soon after my sixteenth birthday I left school. Most of the girls from Church schools left at fourteen but being at the Grammar School I stayed on, as was the norm. I attended night school three nights a week to learn shorthand, typing and book-keeping. My parents paid 5s a lesson. I am very grateful for those chances to learn so much, but at the time I often thought of the girls who were free to 'go out with boys' and so forth.

Back to my childhood! I can remember a typical washing day. The previous evening the home-made rag rugs from the kitchen were lifted, shaken out and put in the shed. Soft water was pumped from the pump in the kitchen to fill the copper which stood in one corner. It took about seven zinc buckets to fill it. Then the sticks and coal were put in the copper fire grate, ready to be lighted around 5.30 the next morning. Mother competed with neighbours in a friendly way, to get lines of snowy washing out as early as possible on Monday mornings. A rather silly idea but vital to them.

Everything was washed in a zinc bath placed in the stone sink, which had one cold brass tap. After rinsing, the washing was put through a hugh cast-iron mangle with big wooden rollers and a large handle which had to be turned to rotate the rollers. The washing was then put into the copper to boil, best linens and cotton whites first, then the coloureds, using plenty of soda and a little Persil. While they were boiling Mum made our breakfast. We fed the chickens and did other chores before going to school, but always got there on time.

After a long boiling, with a kitchen full of steam, a copper stick (cut from a broomstick handle) was used to lift the very hot soapy clothes into the dolly tub. A galvanized tub about 3 ft high and 2 ft across, it was filled with cold water and the clothes were dollied with the dolly pegs, another heavy wooden gadget with three legs on a thick stem and a crossbar handle. It took lots of energy to twist them round and round but it had to be done. Cleanliness was 'next to Godliness', we were always told. The clothes were once again put through the mangle and put into a rinsing bath of yet more water. Then once again through the mangle, then put into a blue bath. This was cold water with a few swishes from a blue bag, a chemical which enabled the whites to look whiter, or so we were told. Once again through the mangle, then 'Robin' starch for tablecloths, tray-cloths, pillowcases and such like. Then after a final run through the mangle came the ritual of hanging out. The sheets must not be hung where they would catch the bushes and only the best linen hung where it could be seen by neighbours. Underwear must be hung discreetly near the doorway. Such Victorian ideals died very slowly, even then our piano had stockings on its legs.

While the washing was being dried everything movable had to be scrubbed. I hated school holidays for this reason. Kitchen table, stools, rolling-pin, breadboard, pantry floor, window-sills and doorsteps were scrubbed, chamber-pots were sterilized with boiling suds from the copper. In fact, this ritual took several hours. We then had bubble and squeak, a fried dinner of Sunday's left over potatoes and cabbage which was quick and easy to prepare, and cold apple pie with no custard to follow. Then it was time to fetch the washing in.

If it was too dry it had to be damped down before folding and mangling to take out some of the creases, carefully of course. With scarcely time to sit down, the cloth and blanket was put on the kitchen table and irons put in front of the fire. About two hours was spent ironing everything, pillowcase ends, towel tapes and even the dusters. We were allowed at an early age to practise on the latter, then on handkerchiefs, to learn not to scorch or dirty the linen – or else! After ironing, the linen was put on to a very large clothes-horse in front of the fire to air. The next evening was spent mending and darning before putting it all away in drawers. Many people today probably can't imagine having to do without their automatic washing-machines and tumble-driers. Of course in winter things were very uncomfortable as everything had to be dried in front of the one open fire. I can still remember Grandma sitting with her shawl over her knees, in front of a steaming clothes-horse. She lived to be seventy-six, so although it was a bit uncomfortable, it obviously didn't do her much harm.

Some families had a pulley over the fireplace, but Mother never allowed this, although it would have helped when my younger sister was a baby. I was twelve years old and I can remember the days of towelling nappies and other garments hanging in front of the fire, day after day.

In those days there was little transport. Apart from the railways, which we used twice yearly, it was Shanks's pony, walking, or perhaps cycling, everywhere. I walked quite a few miles in my younger days and strangely enough I looked forward to these long walks, along country roads with often no houses for long stretches. There was a gypsy encampment with three highly painted vans on the roadside. We passed the time of day and eventually were on chatting terms. Spotlessly clean and nice people, not drop-outs. One day after sitting two hours at the hospital, having pushed my son 5 miles to get there for treatment, they invited me to share a meal with them. I was tired and hungry, so relished the tempting meal they offered, before tramping home to begin my many chores, to catch up on yet another lost day.

The meal was sumptuous; roast hedgehog, skinned and baked in ashes. It tasted like very tender pork. It was served with roast potatoes, no grease, again done in the hot ashes and all washed down with nettle tea. I am a very particular eater in other people's homes, but this meal was a feast indeed These healthy people taught me a great deal about folklore and natural healing remedies. I am still convinced that a washed cut covered by a cobweb will heal quicker than if covered by plasters. Having trained as an SRN

I've done a great deal of comparing and still think the old cures were better and cheaper, in most cases. A drop of brandy was magic, still is, as a stimulant and disinfectant. I well remember once, when abroad, the water being questionable, so I cleaned my teeth with a few drops of the golden liquid, much safer!

Modern times are good in many ways, but I do remember my childhood in the good old days as a very happy, healthy and friendly time.

CHAPTER ELEVEN

SCHOOL-DAYS IN SUFFOLK

Bill Nichols tells his story of school-days and hard work in Suffolk between the wars.

My name is Bill Nichols and I was born on 27 December 1917, at Chapel Lane, Walton, Felixstowe, Suffolk. Father didn't take much to the farm as a young man although he was brought up to farm work. He left the farm and went to work on buildings. After doing different odd jobs he was looking after the horses for Moys, the coal merchants in Felixstowe. He did a coal round and was responsible for the horses; he was a very good horseman. We had a house adjoining the coal yard, which was quite a decent house for those days. There was gas lighting and we had a gas stove, I remember. There was a copper in the kitchen which was very useful for getting hot water for wash-day, bath water and we even cooked Christmas puddings in it.

Mum was a very good cook; she had been in service as a cook to the local doctor before she was married. I remember at weekends, that is to say on the Saturday, we used to have a joint of brisket of beef. There was never anything cooked in our house on a Sunday, except potatoes. We had a hot meal every other day of the week but on Sunday we had cold meat and potatoes. In winter-time we all had porridge in the morning. It was old-fashioned Quaker Oats that had to be made up overnight and cooked for an hour in an old iron saucepan and then heated up again in the morning. That was in the days before Quick Quaker Oats. Another thing we used to have in the winter-time was old-fashioned pea soup. Mother used to make that in the old iron saucepan too. She used to buy some bones, marrow bones, if possible, from the butchers and they would be stewed for hours on end, to get all the goodness out of them. The following day the stew would be as thick as jelly and Mother then added all sorts of vegetables to it, onions and lentils and pearl barley and that would make very good soup. It was one of her stand-bys for really cold weather.

Most of the vegetables came from the allotment. Father had a large allotment and we boys were expected to give a hand with any work that was wanted. Dropping potatoes, picking up potatoes, a bit of hoeing, pulling up weeds, we were expected to help and I think it did us good, too, because that is the way you learn. We did have a little treat now and again if we had been very good on the allotment or doing odd jobs for either of the parents. Dad would occasionally cough up 6d on a Friday night, pay night of course, if he could spare it. Then we would go round to the local grocers for a pound-and-a-half of block dates (they came in half-hundredweight blocks). Mother would share them out for tea round the table and with a good old thick slice of bread and marge, that was lovely, a real treat.

In the summer-time the treat would be shrimps for tea. Old 'Shrimp Brown' used to come round with his bike, two baskets – fore and aft – and measure out the shrimps by the pint or the half-pint. They were really fresh. He used to bring them straight up from the docks, buying them off the boat, and they were good.

Of course, money was a real problem in those days. Clothes especially were a problem. There were several of us in the family and Mother couldn't buy new clothes, hardly ever. What she did was to go round the jumble sales and buy up a decent piece of material, like perhaps a coat or a suit. Providing the material was good it didn't matter about the size or anything else. If she wanted some trousers for us boys she would then take a pair of our trousers to pieces, undo the seams and cut out a pattern from the new material, laying the old ones on top and cutting round them. If you wanted it a little bit bigger you cut round a bit wider and then with her old sewing-machine she would sew them up and make us a new pair of trousers. She was very good like that and, in fact, it was the only way you could get clothes as there was no money to buy new ones. Shoes had to be bought but they were mended and mended again. Dad always did his own repairs for his own boots and sometimes did ours but occasionally they had to go to the shoe-makers over the road because he could make a far better job of them if they were getting badly worn.

Saturday night was always bath night and the old tin bath was brought in from the yard, where it hung the rest of the week. It was put in the kitchen in front of the copper for the hot water to be ladled out into the bath, and it all made a very cosy bathroom. Of course, there were no bathrooms in hardly any houses then.

On Saturday evenings all boots had to be cleaned, polished nicely and set under the table ready for Sunday morning. Of course, we were always brought up to attend Sunday school. For our part we were brought up to attend the Salvation Army Sunday school. I say boots because there were no shoes in those days for children. If there were we never saw any. We always had boots, boys and girls alike.

We used to enjoy going to Sunday school but I remember once we were rather naughty. It was a beautiful summer's morning, the sun was shining, a really wonderful day and we thought it would be lovely to be out across the fields. No sooner thought of than done. Away we went for about a mile-and-a-half across the fields to a place called Camlet, where there was a beautiful sandy-bottomed stream. We enjoyed a very good paddle there that morning, thoroughly enjoyed it, but then the thought came to us about getting our star cards marked. At Sunday school you had a card and they marked a star in it if you were present. At the end of the year the stars were counted up. If a star was missing, of course, your parents would want to know why. I am afraid we were rather wicked that morning, but the thought came to us that we would have to mark them ourselves. It so happens that if you remove the petals from the outside of the poppy there is a beautiful little black star in the middle with black pollen, and if you pressed that on the card it made a perfect copy of the star that was in the book. I am afraid we used it that Sunday morning and away we went home. Of course, we were found out and we got wrong (into trouble) but we did enjoy that Sunday morning.

We started school at five years old and had a mile to walk each day. That meant a mile in the morning, home to dinner and back in the afternoon and back at night, a total of 4 miles a day. They tell me I was a very chubby boy when I started school but I very soon ran some of that off. More often than not, of course, we were running rather than walking. I cannot remember much about life in the younger classes but I can remember the older classes. It was a good school, the teachers were strict and the headmaster was very strict, but he was very fair. We had to be in the gate before the bell stopped ringing at 9 o'clock. It started ringing at five minutes to nine, so you had warning coming along the road and if you were not inside the gate by the time the bell stopped, you were automatically sent to the headmaster's office. If you were sent there for being late it meant a stroke of the cane, there was no hesitation. You were late and that was that. No excuses!

In the winter-time we had slides across the concrete playground and the headmaster would join in, leading the way down the slides, some of them were 20 or 30 yd long. Beautiful slides they were, but of course we were not supposed to slide, not by rights, because of wearing your boots out, but we did have a turn now and then. In the bad weather when the snow was on the ground this headmaster, Mr Richards, would bring a real sledge down to Peewit Hill, near where we lived, and very often we would be given a ride down the hill in his sledge. He would take about three or four of us at a time. It was beautiful sledge, professionally made, and we did enjoy it for a real treat.

As I say, Mr Richards was really strict and he had a wonderful cure for bad language. Bad language was very rare in those days, it just wasn't done, but if anyone was found out at it his cure was to send the culprits down to the wash-house with the prefects who had to wash out their mouths with carbolic soap. We never knew anyone to go twice. It was a cure, no doubt about that.

For sports at school we played football in the winter-time and we played two or three weeks of cricket and then, as soon as the weather was warm enough, it was swimming. Being about within a mile off the sea it was expected we should learn to swim, quite right too. So on sports afternoon we marched down to the sea front, where the council bathing place was, and there we learnt to swim. Mr Merton, known as Froggy Merton, was a very good swimmer and he would line us all up, about forty boys. We would line up on the beach in a row, he would get in the middle and when he gave the word, we would all dash down head first into the water. It might seem a bit strange everyone doing so at the same time but, you see, if you are just behind the row, you find yourself diving onto other people's heels, which can be very uncomfortable. So you are all trying to keep in the row and keep up, then you have clear water to go into. If the tide was high it was rather deep water to go into, so we had to be a bit careful. But on any but the top of the tide, or on low tide, it was real fun and we could go out up to our chest and practise. Then when Froggy Merton thought you could swim enough or got near to swimming, he would take each one of us in turn and try you out. You would get passed if you could do about five or six strokes. His way was to take each one out beyond their depth and turn them towards the shore with one hand underneath them. Then he would say, 'Right, away you go', take his hand away and you swam to shore. That is a bit of a rough way perhaps of learning, but we learnt. Of course, learning to swim in the sea, where there were often quite fair waves, we did become proficient at dealing with sea swimming. In fact, a lot of us boys belonged to the junior section of the Felixstowe Swimming Club. I can remember times when we came away from the school swimming, walked along the Prom, went to the swimming club and had another swim before we went home. We did like our swim.

We had a good sports day every summer, usually on the town ground. We also went for games and sports on Empire Day, and on Armistice Day we always had a parade in the playground, where the flag was hoisted on the flag-pole and we had a short service. Another thing we did was gardening. Mr Merton was the man in charge of all the gardens too. He was very strict but highly respected. If anyone hung their tools up at the end of a lesson that weren't really polished up, or if he saw any dirt at all on one of them, everyone had to stay until the culprit was found. They were cleaned and put back properly and then the class was dismissed. In that way we learned and you didn't skip your work more than once.

I enjoyed school and my lessons, especially arithmetic. I got on very well at that and found it very interesting. Exams were at the end of each year, and the last two or three years I finished up about third in the class for the general exams and for the eleven plus I finished about seventh out of fifty. I was satisfied at that. I knew that there was only one place to go for and had I won, I couldn't have gone because we couldn't afford it. Grammar school needed a lot of money for uniform and so forth. We just couldn't do it. One of my mates came first, his aunt was a schoolteacher and gave him a lot of help. I noticed that some of the questions on the exam papers were on subjects we had never heard of, so we didn't really have a very good chance.

The last two years I was at school I did a paper round; you had to get something to pay for your boots. The rate then was about 3s 6d a week but I managed to get 4s from W.H. Smith. It was quite a large round covering a large area. After a few months they needed a fresh barrow boy. That is to say to go from the shop to the wholesalers, a matter of about a couple of hundred yards away, early in the morning. I had to bring the papers down from the wholesalers to the sorting room at the back of the shop. That meant starting at half-past six instead of seven o'clock and there was an extra 6*d* a week on your wages. That worked out at a penny a morning, which I reckon was not overpaid for the extra half an hour. I earned that penny a morning. We also collected the money on the Saturday morning and if anyone should be tuppence or threepence short on the money they collected in, when you had added up the books, you just lost it off your wages. My word, that was the way to learn, you counted very carefully then.

I left school as soon as I was fourteen. Of course, in the early 1930s jobs were very scarce, it was a case of you must get something. There was not many jobs to be had at all. I should have gone to the Post Office, I had my name down for a telegram boy, which led to being a postman but my cousin got the job. I found afterwards his father had a word with the postmaster the night before. Not very fair, but still!

I got a job at a local bicycle shop, 10*s* a week. That meant mending punctures, cleaning bikes, doing all sorts of odd jobs and then I learnt the job of changing single-speed bikes to three-speed bikes. You take the hind wheel and cut out the hub, put in new spokes and a new three-speed hub, reassemble the wheel, true the wheel, and then have it checked. Finally the boss or the mechanic would run his eye over it. This was a thing done quite a bit then because three-speed bikes were just coming into favour and it wasn't a great deal of expense to have it done. That was a job I spent quite a bit of time doing the next year. Then, unfortunately, so many firms went out of business and went bankrupt, because as I said times were hard in the early thirties.

I got odd jobs for the next year or so and then my brother decided he would join the Army. He had been working with the cows down on the local farm at Hill House, so I immediately went and saw the farmer and asked if I could have his job. He said, 'Can you get up early in the mornings?'

'Yes Sir', I said.

'Right,' he said, 'Your brother has been a good worker, I'll take a chance on you.' So I started the following Monday. I was then to learn what hard work was.

It meant seven days a week, no such thing as a half-day or day off, of course. We started at 5 o'clock in the morning and we finished at 4 o'clock in the afternoon. The farmer was Mr Forrest, he was a good farmer and a good boss to us, treating us very fairly. We didn't see much of him because he had a lot of business work as well but we got on well with him. He had two farms and three herds of cows. The best herd, all pedigree Friesians, was down at a place called East End Farm. At the other farm there were two herds, one of Friesians, mostly pedigree, some of them came from East End of course, and the other was a small herd of pedigree Jerseys. The Friesians grazed down on the marshes, a good half-mile away down what we called 'The Drift'. It was an old rough roadway with trees each side meeting over the top. The Jerseys grazed on the Brick Hill meadows about half a mile in the other direction.

There were three of us milking. Old Billy looked after the dairy and the calves, Curly, his son, mixed the feed and so on, and I was helping the boss's son carting straw, hay and bringing all the stuff that was needed for the herds. Then in the summer-time there would be oats etc. to be cut. We had to get a load each day for the cows, which meant mowing and we soon had our own scythe. Sometimes in later summer there was the maize to harvest. That grew up about 6 or 7 ft and whereas we could cart the oats on the tumbril, the maize we had to cart on a light wagon. We had a ladder to carry the maize up on the wagon and if there was a wetter job than that, I don't know what is as maize holds a tremendous lot of water. Sugar-beet tops were used the early part of the winter but they were usually carted for us. You have to be very careful with sugar-beet tops because they will put cows off their milk in a matter of a day if they get too many of them in a short time. You have to start them gradual and build up. In the winter there was mangel beet to cart as well. They were fed raw on the field. The cows cut them themselves but for the horses they were put through the cutter and mixed in with the feed.

In the mornings after the milking it was my job to take the milk down to the dairy, which was also run by our boss. This was in Felixstowe and it meant a journey of about a mile-and-a-half with an old mare and an old milk float, taking a couple of churns down to the dairy. I could just about get back in time to go to breakfast. We had breakfast about nine each morning and then carried on with the other work after breakfast. In the winter it could be a rum old job going down into town with the old mare because very often the frost came down in the morning after about half-past seven and you could find yourself on a road, quite a wet road, and then go another half a mile and find yourself on ice. So in the winter-time I always had to carry studs and a studding iron and hammer in order that I could stop along the road somewhere and 'rough up', as we called it, on the way down to the dairy. That wasn't a very handy sort of job. It meant putting studs in the mare's shoes, which had holes put in them when they were made.

About that time I had a lesson on the art of catching hares, poaching really I suppose. I had been on the stack getting some hay, we had to cut it with stack knives of course. I happened to look down the lane and I could see Curly on the marshes as he had gone to look at some heifers. He was walking about with his stick over his shoulder, which I thought was unusual. I saw him go in almost a circle, make a stroke on the ground and pick up what appeared to be a rabbit and then come home. I saw him a little later on and said, 'Hello Curly, did you get a rabbit this morning?' He looked at me and laughed, 'Did you see me?'

'Yes,' I replied.

He said, 'Well boy, I'll tell you how that's done. It was a hare and not a rabbit and that is classed as game and I shouldn't have had it. If ever you see a hare sitting tight on the marsh like that, remember they can't see straight ahead of them. If you do see one sit there tight in the form, walk round till you come up to it right head-on and give it a sharp tap behind its ears with your stick. But when you pick it up, pick it up all four legs at once. Then, if anyone like you is watching or an old gamekeeper is watching, it don't hang long like a hare. Carry it all four legs in one hand and it looks like a rabbit at a distance.' I thought that was a good yarn.

CHAPTER TWELVE

EARLY DAYS IN KENT

Mrs K. Chambers writes of her early childhood on a farm in Kent.

I was born in 1926 and my early childhood was spent on a farm in Kent. When I was a year old my grandmother died and so my parents and I and my eight-year-old brother moved in to my grandfather's tied cottage, for my mother to 'keep house' for us all, including my father's younger brother. This was at Little Murston, near Sittingbourne, Kent. My grandfather worked as a farm labourer at Youngs' Corner Farm nearby, my uncle being a fruit man on the farm.

Even in those days, when I was still young, I remember my father complaining about the sprays which my uncle used on the fruit trees, saying it weren't right to put poison on and so on.

Of course, there was no gas, electric or water in the cottage. We had oil lamps downstairs and candles when we went to bed. Our water came from a well in the front garden. Used water from the cottage was thrown outside or perhaps used for watering the vegetables, when necessary.

We had a large room, used on Sundays, when my grandfather lit the fire. But weekdays were spent in the kitchen where my mother did all the work, cooking on a 'black kitchener' (enclosed apart from a round grill at the front). There was a table for meals in the centre of the room and a smaller table just inside the door which contained bowls and jugs for washing and washing up. There was a copper in the corner of the room but it wasn't used for washing. My other uncle and aunt took our bed linen and shirts to their farm cottage and brought a brown paper parcel of clean linen the following Sunday.

It was a treat for us to have visitors! I remember at Christmas our copper was used to store the loaves of bread needed to see us over the holiday, when we had other friends visit for tea. In the evenings we played cards, dice and lotto. My father had two mouth-organs and he sang songs such as 'Down at the Old Bull and Bush'. People always asked him to sing and enjoyed it. Such laughter! Being young, I remember it all as being happy times. My birthday being on the 17 December, I think my birthday presents got mixed with Christmas presents and I was thrilled to get a pillowcase of presents waiting on my bed on Christmas morning.

Every year I went just down the road to another small farm, worked by Mr and Mrs Sparks, to watch the shearing of the sheep by hand, in an open shed. It was very exciting!

I also loved to watch the reaper and binder at harvest time in the field adjoining our cottage and every year a 'traveller' known as old 'Sparky' turned up to help with the harvest. I think he lived among the stooks of corn in the field near our cottage and my brother and I took a fat dinner out to him every night and listened to his 'stories', which my brother loved. I was also a little bit afraid of old 'Sparky' in his tattered clothes and so was my mother. The two of us were also scared of the gypsies who came in the horse caravan and stayed near the cottage periodically and came to our well for water.

Our lavatory was a hut in the far corner of the back garden, a long wooden seat with a huge pit underneath. There was a trapdoor outside at the back, where the cesspit was emptied by two men with a horse and cart in the evenings. I was always firmly kept indoors during this time!

My grandfather and his mate spent endless days hoeing in the fields, swedes, turnips, cabbages, and seed sowing with the 'drill'. There was a wagoner, Mr Waters (much respected by my grandfather), who had the horses to look after. There were wagons for harvest, carts for vegetables.

There was great excitement when the rabbits were hiding in the last bit of standing corn in the centre of the field and all 'hands' took dogs or guns, hoping to catch a dinner. I also looked forward to going up to the farm at threshing time. All the men would be working hard and the noisy machines were huge; my grandfather always warned me when the stack was almost finished and all the dogs were getting excited and dancing round to get at the rats and mice! Incidentally, we had to leave the cottage when it was 'condemned' because of the rats. They came out one afternoon and took our bag of Chelsea buns just delivered by the baker and left on the table in our Sunday room. My father was so furious he dug out their hole in the skirting!

I was fascinated by our milk being ladled out from the churn into our jugs. We used to keep it fresh in hot weather by standing it in water with white muslin over the top. It always 'turned' when we had a storm! And oh! the smell and taste of rancid butter! Oil and candles came in a van with a most peculiar smell.

Mother and I went shopping to Sittingbourne on Saturdays with friends in their pony and trap. The pony was left in stalls at the back of The Lion in the High Street, an old coaching inn with a cobbled yard through the archway entrance. These friends were from Elmley Ferry, where the eldest man was a ferryman; the father had died. Every Sunday my mother and I went there for tea. We had a great time; there were five boys and five girls in that large family.

When our cottage was condemned we were moved to a much bigger and better farmhouse, dated 1614 in brass old-fashioned figures over the huge fireplace. It was red brick and had bay windows with a huge scullery, brick floored at the back, and a huge stone sink. It was from the farmhouse that I once saw the enormous Aurora Borealis from the window.

My grandfather still worked on the same farm. We still had no mod-cons, other than a china-type lavatory pan under a wooden seat, but we had to take buckets of water to flush it down. One time, our neighbours in the other half of the farmhouse had a flooded cellar and the men from three families all came on a Saturday afternoon to dig a very deep ditch as a soak-away down the length of our very long garden. There were no more floods after that!

We were pleased to have a huge walnut tree in our garden, as well as pear and apple trees. Most of the farm buildings were unused there, except for a newer barn; a walled garden and long greenhouse were completely unused, which seems rather a shame now. Sadly we were unable to stay there very long as the farming owners were changed just before the 1939 war and West Forge Farm, including our house, was sold off and we had to move. We were all very sad. My grandfather continued working at the same farm, but we were moved to another tied cottage at Murston, where my father now worked as a brick-worker labourer. Then, of course, the war changed everything (or almost).

I realize now that it must have been very hard work for the family, but being so young I was very happy and had a wonderful time. I remember my mother making flannel 'undershirts' for my father and grandfather, sewing by hand in herring-bone stitch, which I also helped sew when I was older. The men tied string round their waists and sacks around their legs, and they put sacks round their shoulders when it rained. They always wore caps of course. They wore trousers with a flap at the front instead of the normal fly buttons, and they always said 'thank 'ee'.

During the early 1930s, a 'treat' for Mother and me was to see the Tickham Hunt meet just below the cottage a few times in the season. At that time we went to school by horse and covered van. All the children from the farms and the Grensden family from Elmley Island came over by ferry boat to get to Murston School. Sadly the Grensdens lost a daughter, drowned in the River Swale. One girl from Horty Ferry came by pony to the Grensden Farm, then by boat to school but she didn't come in the bad winter weather. Later Mr Freddle Sales got a new car and we were taken to school in that.

CHAPTER THIRTEEN

A BAPTIST MINISTER'S DAUGHTER

Olive Evans writes of her early life in the Rhondda Valley at the start of the century.

I was born in February 1901 in Pentre, Rhondda, where my father was a Welsh Baptist minister. I already had a brother, aged four, and a sister, aged two. We lived in a very nice four-bedroomed house in a quiet street on a hill.

The Rhondda Valley was the place of the coal-mines and most of the men were coal-miners. We saw them come home covered with coal dust. When they reached home they bathed in a tin bath in front of the kitchen fire. The wives usually had to boil the water and carry it in buckets to the bath. Many a time when I was very young I would wander into a neighbour's house and see the man and sometimes sons bathing in front of a fire. I wondered why they didn't go to the bathroom, as we at home did, but most houses in those early days had no bathrooms.

Gas was the only mode of lighting in those early days. We used to watch the street lamp-lighters come along with their long poles which they would push up under the glass lampshades to lift the switch which would then change the tiny pilot light into a bright light. Then, when daylight came, along would come the lamp-lighter and reverse the procedure.

We had gaslight in the house but the cooking was done in the oven of the coal grate – black and probably made of steel and iron. It was a closed grate with two removable rings which had to be taken off when the kettle or saucepans had to be boiled. We had a boiler behind the fire so we had plenty of hot water.

We had a wonderful mother. She worked so hard keeping everything shining like glass. We had linoleum on the floors with occasional mats or rugs in places. These had to be taken out to the back yard and put on a line or wall to be brushed with a hard bristle hand brush. The floors would be swept with a long handled soft bristle brush.

My mother used to make our dresses and coats. She used a Singer treadle machine to stitch the seams after she had tacked the cut-out pieces.

She also made her own bread. My sister and I used to go down to the main road where tramcars on tramlines were the means of transport right down the valley. We had railway stations too. When we got to the main road we made our way to the local brewery where we had our jug filled with 'balm'. I do not know whether or what we had to pay for this. (I gather that balm was yeast in those days.)

Mother would mix the flour, salt and balm together until it became a pliable soft dough, then she would divide it and put the dough into greased tins and placed our special mark (with the tip of a large dinner knife) and that was our mark. The tins would then be put on the rack above the grill so that the dough would rise. When the loaves were almost twice the size, we would take the bread to the bake-house not far away. Later my sister and I would go to fetch the bread and I was always fascinated to see how, at just one glance at us, the lady would bring us our loaves from probably dozens of other people's bread.

On Sundays my father wore a top hat and morning coat with its wide shiny lapels and a slit down the back, which ended at the

Mrs Owen as a child with her family, c. 1905. Mrs Owen is sitting behind her sister, on the right

waist with two small black buttons. Father kept his red silk handkerchief in the pocket of one side of the slit. We had to cross the main road to get to the opposite side and to our chapel. Invariably we met the church organist, a Mr Tapper Jones, crossing the road to his church. He too in morning coat and top hat. His little son, Sidney (who later became Town Clerk of Cardiff), wore what I thought was an Eton suit. Whether this was so I do not know. Strangely enough, after ninety years I suddenly remembered that our next-door neighbour, Mr Salter, who was a schoolteacher, also wore morning dress to go to church.

The chapel played a large part in our lives. We went three times on Sunday and every seat would be full. My father was a very well-known preacher and would preach a sermon for forty to fifty minutes and towards the end he would get into 'hwyl' as we say in Welsh and would sing-song the last part. All Welsh preachers would do this. The practice died out in the 1940s and '50s, although many older people still remember the 'hwyl'.

In winter we used to go to the chapel vestry for all kinds of meetings and very well attended they would be. The older ones had Bible readings and discussions while we children would learn to recite a psalm or words of a Welsh hymn (I can still recite them). There would be little homely competitions where we competed by singing or reciting. We had children's choirs too. We sang after learning the piece by solfa (not by reading old notation) and a modulator.

As children we read any books we could get hold of and I still think that our generation had no problems with spelling as continuous reading instinctively taught us how to spell. We played indoor board games – ludo, snakes and ladders and many more. Outdoor games had their seasons. We played with skipping ropes and did all sorts of tricks with them. Then we played 'Cattie and Doggie' – bowling a hoop (doggie) along the road or pavement with a stick (cattie) without letting the hoop fall. We also played hopscotch – kicking a small flat stone from one square into another in as few strokes as possible. I remember keeping empty cocoa tins and knocking two holes into the end of each one and then tying a cord on to each tin. Then by holding a cord in each hand and placing a foot on each tin I could walk tall. Marbles came later but those were boys' games.

We also had a great game called 'buttons'. We drew a round ring about a yard in diameter on the pavement, and we each put in the same number of any kind of button. Then 3 or 4 yd away we drew a line (usually with chalk). We each had a 'dummy'. This was half of a ring from a baby's dummy. It was made of bone then. Standing at the line we started drawing the dummy towards the ring with the tips of our fingers. This was not so easy as it sounds as the dummy was a funny shape and would not always go the way one wanted! The first to get her dummy into the ring would then proceed to pick up with her thumb (usually wetted with spit!) as many buttons as she could without dropping one. We had hand-made cotton bags with string threaded through the top hem and hung around our necks to keep the buttons in.

Going down to the grocer's shop was a joy. It was usually a large room with a well-scrubbed wooden counter all round. Flour, dried fruit and sugar were sold 'loose'. The weighing scale with its brass pan and brass weights stood on the counter and with a scoop the grocer would weigh the amount one needed and put it in a blue bag. Sugar was usually put in a blue bag which was made of a paper similar to blotting paper. Butter was kept in a tub and with two wooden pats was shaped into an oblong block and wrapped in white paper, obviously not in greaseproof paper. The only tins I can remember were those of cocoa, and Camp coffee in bottles. Salt was sold in blocks. Tea was kept in large labelled tins.

There were greengrocer shops where one could buy sweets. These were kept in large glass bottles. I cannot remember how they sold chocolates – there were no packaged sweets as far as I can remember.

A Baptist Minister's Daughter

When we were taken by train to the seaside we had to go to our nearest station, Treorchy, and we travelled in trains made up of similar carriages with doors at each end. The top half of the door was a window which could be lifted up or dropped by means of a wide leather strap. I always remember that after passing through the third station and just before we entered a well-known tunnel, our parents would hurriedly drop the window down so that we could all inhale the smoke and fumes of the engine inside the tunnel. It was supposed to be 'good for our chests'. I can almost smell the sulphur to this day.

I do not remember much of my school-days in Pentre. Our teachers in the girls' school always wore skirts to the ground and high-necked blouses. They always wore their hair with a knot on the top of the head. I remember one teacher always pinned a piece of white paper over the bottom half of her sleeves to keep them clean. A teacher in those days had to give up teaching when she got married.

Everything seems to be so easy nowadays. I remember my mother having to do all the washing in a big tub or zinc bath. She had a scrubbing board, part of which was corrugated brass, on which she had to rub up and down (with common household soap) each garment until it was clean. Then when clothes – frocks, pinafores, shirts, etc. – had to be ironed, Mother had to bring out two heavy irons. These were heated on the hotplate of our grate or on the open fire and then the irons had to be cleaned before attempting the ironing. I think the ironing was done on the kitchen table and I cannot remember having an ironing stand as we have nowadays.

Ladies used to wear beautiful frocks down to the floor with lots of pleats and lace and bows. The hats were large and high. In summer they would be trimmed heavily with bows of silk or satin and artificial flowers. In winter the trimmings on the hats were usually of feathers and plumes and were very heavy on the head.

The Rhondda and other valleys in Glamorgan are now very different from our days. There are no coal-mines and the hills and old tips of coal rubbish which had been dumped there are now landscaped and very beautiful.

When I was twelve years old Father accepted a 'call' to a large chapel in a lovely village in rural Carmarthenshire where life changed dramatically – no electricity, no gas, no running water.

When I used to stay with friends in a farm not far from Conwy (Gwynedd) in the 1920s and '30s, they made their own bread but these were not baked in the kitchen oven. Out in the farmyard there was a small stone building. On one side there was a large oven door and when the door was opened it revealed a huge square-sided hole. In the morning they would light a fire in this and then keep it burning with logs or branches and trunks of dead trees and as these burned someone would always come along and put more fuel on and in the fire. Later, the housewife knew exactly when the oven was ready – the fire dying out and the base of the oven swept clean of the wood ash. Then the huge loaves of oven-ready bread would be brought out and placed in the oven. The oven door was then closed. It had no chimney and again the housewives knew exactly when the bread was ready and it would be brought out, beautifully baked. Every loaf would have to be scraped of the ash that sometimes clung to the loaves, but what delicious bread it was!

I remember how we were taught solfa in the girls' school. There was a modulator hanging on the board and easel and it was a long narrow one – cream with black printed DOH, RAY, ME, FAH, SOH, LA, TE, DOH starting from the bottom. The teacher with her pointer would start at the bottom DOH, which we dutifully sang and then moved up to RAY and so on to top DOH. When we could sing it through she would then point at the notes at random, missing one or two notes out, and thus we sang. Sometimes we sang a tune that we already knew. We had a singing lesson of half an hour every week.

Milk was delivered by horse and carriage, the milkman bringing to each house a can of about 4 gallons and with a pint measure he would pour out the necessary amount into your jug. This method was still used in the early 1940s.

CHAPTER FOURTEEN

ODD ONE OUT

In drawing this work to a conclusion I take the liberty of including some account of my own experiences of childhood on a farm in the 1920s and '30s. It was the memory of these experiences that led me to initiate the collection of reminiscences that have formed the basis of this series of books.

I was born on 8 August 1923 in the midst of a heatwave and I am told that wet sheets were hung around the room to keep my mother cool. I was delivered by an old lady, the wife of a local greengrocer, who doubled as a midwife. My parents lived in one of a row of semi-detached cottages at Northall Green, Dereham, Norfolk. These were tied cottages belonging to the farmer who owned Hoe Lodge Farm on which my maternal grandfather, Walter Pitcher, worked. There was a shortage of housing at the time and my parents lived with my mother's parents. My father, William, worked for about eight months a year at Smith's Maltings in the market town of Dereham. The maltings closed in the summer and then Father worked on the farm.

When I was three months old, my grandfather was asked to go and work on a farm at Beetley which his employer had just acquired. The accommodation there was in the farmhouse which had been divided into two cottages. So at Michaelmas we moved into Tarn Farm, and my first memories are of that house. It was a plain redbrick eighteenth-century farmhouse, and our section consisted of a large kitchen/dining-room in which we mainly lived, and a sitting-room which was reserved for Sundays and special occasions. There had been another room downstairs but the floor had been taken out and we used that as a storeroom and shed. Upstairs were two bedrooms and a large box-room over the shed, and I loved to get into that room to play on wet days.

My story can hardly be typical for I was brought up an only child in an unusual family of parents and grandparents. I was shy and seldom had other children to play with since my mother considered most of the village children to be unsuitable playmates.

My grandfather was illiterate but Grandmother and my parents liked reading and had a small collection of books, which, in addition to the Bible, hymn books and some religious novels, included the autobiography of George Edwards, founder of the Agricultural Workers' Union, and Fred Henderson's *The Case for Socialism*. These books gave me my first introduction to socialism and trade unionism. The collection also included a biography of Queen Victoria (a school prize awarded to my mother for needlework) and some Victorian school textbooks and children's books.

We took the Labour newspaper *The Daily Herald*, a religious weekly, *The Sunday Companion*, and the monthly journal of the Agricultural Workers' Union, *The Landworker*, in its distinctive deep red cover. I was read to, and taught to read for myself before going to school, and regularly read *The Chick's Own*, a comic for the very young.

The first event I can distinctly remember was falling off a gate when I was three. It was a large five-barred gate at the entrance to the farmyard. I was not allowed to climb it, but when Grandmother was not looking, I did. The gate was not properly fastened and swung open throwing me onto the sharp flints of the yard. My forehead was badly cut.

Other memories of the period before going to school included Grandmother taking me to play in a pine wood where there was a tree whose branches swept to the ground forming a sort of tent in which I played Red Indians. Much of my play was purely imaginative for I had no playmates.

I had many toys, including dolls and teddies and I would load these into a large wooden pedal car that an uncle had made and drive it round the garden paths.

On summer days an ice-cream cart would sometimes come out from the town. This cart was made of wood painted white and yellow and was drawn by a pony.

On Fridays we usually went to market in Dereham in a bus which only ran on market-days. It was a red single-decker and usually driven by a lady. One day it was involved in an accident. A motorist overtook the bus and cut in too quickly forcing the bus into the ditch. Luckily no one was hurt, but this provided one of the few moments of real excitement I can remember from that period.

There was a small flower garden outside our front door with rose bushes, lavender and flower beds edged with stones and shells which always reminded me of the nursery rhyme, 'Mary, Mary quite contrary', though I couldn't find the 'silver bells' or 'the pretty maids all in a row'. However, the garden became infested with ants and one day I went out with Grandad to kill the ants by pouring paraffin over the nest. At the end of the house was a long garden which was mainly used for growing potatoes and other vegetables, though the end nearest the house was devoted to growing sweet peas, flowers that my father loved.

On the left-hand side was a chicken house and run, while at the far end was a small wood, separated from the garden by a thick hedge. I was forbidden to enter the wood but for me it became a magical place peopled with little folk and strange creatures.

At the age of five I was sent to school at North Elmham some two miles up the main road. There was little traffic at that time but my mother took me in the morning and fetched me home in the afternoon. She seemed to fear the tramps and gypsies that sometimes used that road. I remember little of that school for I became ill with rickets and eczema and was off for most of that year. The following year I was sent to Beetley school, which meant travelling almost as far but in a different direction. This school consisted of a large room in which juniors and seniors were taught and a smaller room for the infants. Later on all seniors were transferred to the Central School in Dereham. I remember walking home from school along a lane and turning right at the bottom to watch the blacksmith shoeing horses at his forge. Returning many years later I was led to write this poem:-

School Road

Riding the dusty
western trail from school
white lamped with parsley
wild, often we turned
right into the forge
to watch the blacksmith
flaying iron red
on a cold anvil,
in flight of sparkling
stars. Shaping the shoe
to fit the held roof.

A gentle way with horses
he had, They stood quiet
to his hand, being shoed
for travelling the road.

Half a century gone,
gone blacksmith, gone forge.
White parsley still lights
the pav'd but shrunken road.

At harvest time we took food and drink to Father and Grandfather in the fields. At other times of the year men took their 'elevenses' with them. This was usually bread and cheese and a currant bun which Grandma made; she called them harvest cakes though she made them all year round.

On Saturdays in summer we went down to the meadow by the village pond to watch Father play cricket for the village team. On Sunday afternoons I was taken by my parents to the service at the Primitive Methodist chapel, but I was not sent to Sunday school as that would have been an additional journey. The services were usually taken by local preachers, some of whom created excitement through their enthusiasm, though at the age of six I did not always know what they were talking about. My most vivid memories were of the Sunday school Anniversary, when the chapel was crowded and each child was expected to make a contribution, a recitation or a song, and the harvest festival when the chapel was decked with fruit and flowers and vegetables, with sheaves of corn and loaves of bread forming the centre-piece. After the service there was a harvest tea. My religious preferences were clearly shaped by the informality and enthusiasm of that Methodist chapel.

In many villages there was a great divide between Church and Chapel, between the Anglicans and the Nonconformists. My father had been brought up in the Methodist chapel at Great Ryburgh and my mother was a Congregationalist so I had been christened at the Cowper Congregational church, Dereham, which I attended after the age of seven when we returned to live at Northall Green in 1930. My grandfather's employer needed him to work on the farm at Northall Green so we returned to live in the same row of houses in which I had been born, although not the same house but two doors away at No. 5.

This house was built of red brick and roofed with tiles. The inner walls I think were of clay lump and very thick. Downstairs was a large living-room and behind it the kitchen/dining-room. In the kitchen there was a copper on one side of the fireplace and a wall oven on the other. The fireplace had hobs on which saucepans and kettles could be boiled. There was a large deal table and half a dozen chairs, and just enough room for the five of us to sit for meals. At the end of the kitchen was a pantry, where among other things there were large jars in which eggs were preserved, rows of jam jars and pots of pickles. Buckets of drinking water were kept there since all drinking water had to be carried about 200 yd from the farm. Water for washing was collected from the roof and stored in large butts. In the front room a door opened onto the staircase. Upstairs there were three bedrooms.

The toilet was up the garden. It had a wooden seat above a large bucket which had to be emptied into a hole dug in the garden, which ensured that the crops were well fertilized. Next to the toilet was a shed where coal was kept and bicycles and tools were stored. The shed was never locked but nothing was ever stolen.

There was no electricity or gas so we depended on oil lamps and candles for light and coal fires for warmth. A large oil lamp stood on the table in the front room but the rest of the house was usually lighted with candles. Candles were also kept in the toilet. There was a fireplace in the big bedroom but it was never used. We had a Calor oil heater which was used upstairs in cold weather.

The coal was delivered on horse drawn wagons by men who had to carry the heavy bags round to the back of the houses to the coal shed. Because we used coal fires we had to have the chimneys swept regularly. Ours were swept by Mr 'Dickey' Dodman who lived in London Road. When he arrived the furniture would be covered with sheets and heavy sacking hung over the fireplace. There was a hole in this sacking to allow him to push the brush up the chimney. New lengths of pole were screwed on to extend the pole so that the brush could be pushed all the way up the chimney. When he thought he had nearly reached the top we were asked to go outside to watch the brush emerge from the chimney pot. A few pushes up and down and the chimney was cleaned. The soot was collected in a bag in the hearth. A skilful sweep made very little mess in the house.

To avoid having to pay a sweep some people tried various methods of cleaning the chimney themselves including setting fire to the soot in the chimney, but as this was liable to damage the chimney or even set fire to the house, it was not popular with landlords. The burning soot flying out of the chimney was also likely to set fire to haystacks or crops in the fields and gardens, so this method upset both neighbours and local farmers.

Another method my grandfather tried once was firing a shotgun up the chimney. This was very effective in removing the soot which not only descended on his head but blackened everything in the house. Grandmother did not allow him to use that method again.

We usually ate in the kitchen but on Sundays and when visitors came we had tea in the front room and some of the best china came out.

We ate well. On Saturdays we usually had a large joint of beef served with Norfolk dumplings. Large, soft and white they were delicious and quite unlike the bullet-hard little lumps that are served up as dumplings outside Norfolk today. With these we had whatever vegetables were in season. There were no freezers so the only vegetables that could be obtained out of season were dried peas. These had to be soaked in water overnight but even when cooked they were unappetizing. Overcooked they became 'mushy' peas which have become popular today, much to my amazement. Some vegetables could have been bought in cans but they were too expensive, so we ate what was in season – peas and beans in summer, cabbages, cauliflowers, sprouts, broccoli at other times. Potatoes, carrots, parsnips, turnips could be stored and used all year. For sweets we had apple pies, pumpkin pies, spotted dick, treacle puddings and rice puddings.

Being religious, Mother and Grandmother did not cook on Sundays, so we only had cold meat left over from the Saturday joint, with bread and pickles for dinner. In Norfolk dinner is eaten at midday. The evening meal is tea, though when meat or cooked meat is served it is called high tea.

During the week dinner would be meat puddings or dumplings with vegetables and a sweet. At tea-time there would be bread and jam or cheese, and cake. On Sundays we often had jelly and thought it a great treat. Breakfast would be porridge or cornflakes, bacon and eggs, toast or bread.

Tea was served with all meals. On rare occasions we had coffee. It was Camp coffee, a liquid essence that I thought was horrible. At night we usually had a cup of cocoa or Ovaltine and I was one of the original Ovaltinies and still have the badge I wore. Many products were promoted through 'clubs' for children. Cocoa had a cocoacubs club, and Gibbs dentifrice promoted an Ivory Castles League. I belonged to both.

I attended the National Junior School, Dereham. The headmaster was Mr Lloyd, a fine man. This was a mixed school, but the sexes were segregated at playtime, with separate playgrounds for boys and girls. The boys tended to divide into two gangs each with its own territory at opposite ends of the playground and there were frequent fights over incursions into the other gang's territory. Fights were relatively mild affairs in those days since they were restricted to the use of fists only. No one ever thought of using a weapon or of kicking an opponent when he was down. Such behaviour was unfair, unBritish and branded you as a 'Dago'. These rules were generally accepted throughout society. I was a working-class boy in a school that was predominantly working class, so there was no question of the norms of our childhood being middle class. Of course there were always some boys who did not conform, but they were sorted out by their fellow pupils before the adults found out.

These rules applied also in the senior school, though there was some bullying. As a small fat boy I was subjected to much ragging and mockery but very little physical abuse.

In my first year at junior school I was in Miss Curtis's class, a kind lady who introduced me to the world of literary fantasy by reading *The Wind in the Willows* to the class. I was delighted with that book and persuaded my mother to buy a paperback copy which in a tattered condition still sits on my library shelf. I must have read it hundreds of times.

Another teacher feared for her strictness taught music but my clearest memory of her is of learning carols to sing at the Christmas service as the school was a Church of England establishment. In particular I enjoyed singing 'Little Town of Bethlehem'.

I disliked school, not because of the teachers but because I did not get on well with other children. Consequently I made every possible excuse to stay away. I did not play truant for fear of the truancy officers, whom we called 'Kid Catchers', but was able to persuade my mother that I was sick so that she would send a note to the teachers. My mother was over-protective, as is often the case with only children, so it was very easy to persuade her. The result of not attending was that I was always near the bottom of the class, and I was therefore not entered for the scholarship examinations for entry to the grammar school. There were only a few free places in local grammar schools in those days, so at the age of eleven I went to the senior elementary school in Crown Road. This was known as the Central School because it provided for children from the villages as well as from the town itself.

When I was about eleven my father bought me a second-hand bike and I learned to ride, with many a harmless fall in the grassy lanes near home. I now rode to school each day but left my bike at the house of a friend who lived near the school as Father was worried that the bike might be stolen or damaged if left in the school yard.

As a result of the fact that I had suffered from a double hernia since the age of seven I had to wear a truss until I was judged to be healed at the age of sixteen. This disability restricted my physical activities throughout my childhood. I was not allowed to lift heavy objects or to play strenuous games. The only game I was allowed to play at school was cricket, a game which I also played with my father and other children on a meadow near home. Because of my defective sight, however, I was never a very good batsman. I was disappointed in my ambition to emulate my hero, Jack Hobbs. My shortsightedness had been detected when I was seven and from that time I have always worn spectacles. My further problem of red-green colour-blindness was not discovered until I was a student at Liverpool University.

As I grew older my reading interests widened. I was introduced to poetry by a teacher, Harold Whitby. One of our text books was *The Way of Poetry*, edited by John Drinkwater. I was also introduced to Shakespeare and Dickens in his class. I saved my pocket-money to buy second-hand books. When I had saved enough I would take a bus to Norwich and spend the day searching the many second-hand bookshops to be found there. Good books could be found for 6*d* and old classics in a worn condition for a penny. In this way I soon acquired a representative collection of the major poets and novelists. Woolworths sold 6*d* copies of Dickens novels; they also sold American science fiction magazines such as *Astounding S.F.* and *Weird Tales*. My first introduction to science fiction had been through the *Modern Boy* magazine which carried a series of stories featuring the character of Captain Justice. My parents encouraged my reading habits and there was another source of cheap books of which we made use. The *Daily Herald* offered a wide range of books to readers who collected coupons published in the paper, and in this way we acquired books covering a wide range of topics, including Bernard Shaw's *Complete Plays*, Churchill's *The World Crisis*, an atlas, and books on history, wildlife, science, economics, psychology, as well as gardening and handicrafts. I became particularly interested in science and read a magazine called *The Modern World* and pursued my interest in wildlife through the *Naturelover* magazine.

I was also a regular visitor to the local library and largely self taught, like many of my generation who were denied access to the grammar school system. Indeed it was probably because I read for interest and not because of the pressures of a formal education that my interests spread so widely and my enthusiasm for learning persisted.

My interests, however, were by no means restricted to reading. I spent much of my spare time wandering around the fields and lanes observing wildlife, usually on my own, and learned to identify most of the plants, birds and animals living in that part of Norfolk. I collected birds' eggs (only taking one of each species) and built up a collection of pressed flowers to help with identification.

I also collected stamps and cigarette cards, and constructed working models with Meccano and one Christmas I was given a model stationary steam-engine which could be used to drive the models I made. I was also interested in railways and in addition to watching the train that passed the bottom of our garden I had a set of Hornby trains. Most of my interests could be pursued alone, but I had some close friends. Alan lived just down the road, but Gary lived at Wroxham although he frequently came to Dereham for long stays with his aunt. He was very scientifically minded and we sometimes made gunpowder and stink bombs which upset my mother.

By the time I was thirteen my record at school had improved. I attended more regularly and was top of the class in most subjects. My parents and the headmaster, Mr Walter Tebbitt, wanted me to stay on after my fourteenth birthday. I stayed on until the term before I was fifteen in the summer of 1938. My first job was as an errand boy for Mr Robinson who had a chemist shop in the market-place. Then, early in 1939, I took up poultry keeping. I had always helped look after the poultry which we kept in our garden and Father and Grandfather decided they would help me by expanding the size of the flock. A friend who owned a small farm allowed us to keep our poultry on a small meadow and I continued to do this for eight years. In 1940 at the age of sixteen I joined the Home Guard which I stayed with until it was disbanded. When called up for National Service I was rejected on medical grounds.

Shopping

Supermarkets are claimed to be a convenient way of shopping but in many ways shopping was easier in the 1930s. You could walk up to the counter in a grocer's shop and ask the assistant for what you wanted. She would fetch it; there was no searching the shelves for ages only to find that the shop did not stock it. When your order was made up you paid the assistant – no queueing at the check-out. In many shops your order would be packed up and delivered to your door so there was no problem of getting your goods home if you didn't have transport. If you lived in the country the town grocers would send a salesman each week to collect your order, and the goods would be delivered the next day. The salesman who came to collect our order, Mr 'Totty' Wright, was a real character, a friendly man full of jokes and stories who always seemed to have a cigarette hanging from the corner of his mouth. Sitting in the kitchen with a cup of tea he reminded Mother of all the goods the shop sold and told her of any new lines that had come in. He wrote down the order as she gave it and at the end he would say, 'Are you sure you haven't forgotten anything, Mrs N.?' Sometimes he brought samples, and since we had few sweets I remember the day he brought some Aero chocolate. 'A new line just on the market,' he said. Mother bought a bar.

Most other types of shop provided delivery services and one of the most familiar sights was that of the errand boy on his bike hurrying to deliver goods to some customer's door. Bakers, butchers and fishmongers provided a mobile service with horse-drawn carts and later with motor vans.

Today the customers have to do all the work themselves. Possibly they might pay a bit less but even that is doubtful as supermarkets are usually in a monopolistic position, the small stores having been put out of business in many places.

All the shops had their own distinctive smells. The grocers was a regular perfumery for few goods came pre-packed. If you wanted a quarter-pound of tea the grocer scooped the tea out of a large wooden tea-chest in which it was delivered, weighed it on his scales and wrapped it in paper which often had his name printed on it. The speed and skill with which the goods were wrapped was fascinating to watch.

Hardware shops smelt of oil, paraffin and paint. The floors of butchers' and fishmongers' shops were covered with fresh sawdust, the scent of which mingled with that of the goods they sold.

On market-day we went into town in the donkey cart which we stabled at the blacksmiths. Here were the smells of horses and, if a horse was being shoed, the sharp scent of burnt horse hooves as the blacksmith tried the hot shoe for size before finally nailing it on. The blacksmith was also a wheelwright and sometimes we would find him making a new wooden wheel or fitting a new iron tyre to the wheel. The metal tyre was made to size, heated to make it expand, then placed on the wooden wheel so that as it contracted it fitted tightly. The smell of hot iron and scorched wood mingled with the fumes of his forge. The scents of childhood always evoke memories: the ripe corn in the harvest field, autumn leaves scuffled by our boots as we went down the lane, warm milk straight from the cow, mown hay, leather harnesses in the stable, the smell of hot oil and steam from the threshing engine, the sow nursing her piglets, apples and pears eaten from the tree. All provoke vivid memories.

Here and There

My wife has reminded me of a number of points that have not been covered in the previous accounts. She points out that in infant schools in the 1930s children learned to write with chalk on little blackboards, and of course a few years earlier they would have used slates and written with slate pencils. At the age of seven she learned to knit, making square dusters for use with these blackboards. If they behaved all week infants were allowed to push back their desks and play on Friday afternoons. She remembered dancing to 'A hunting we will go'. She also remembered that when she was six she had been very frightened by a teacher who, when a girl had been too talkative, held up a piece of string and a pair of scissors and threatened to cut out that girl's tongue. Her sister, however, remembered that same teacher with affection for the kindness she had shown when she was suffering with earache.

The surface of the playground was very rough and there were many cut knees. Teachers used old sheets or pillowcases brought by children from home to make bandages.

Parents were often worried about the need to take children to the doctors because of the expense and used many home remedies. For example, a remedy for earache was a flannel bag filled with salt and warmed by the fire. The bag was then tied round the head to cover the ear. Doctors often realized that some parents could pay little. In one case where a small girl from a poor family was bitten by an alsatian dog belonging to a wealthy family the doctor sent his bill to the dog's owner. Children often had camphor balls hung round their necks to ward off disease and some children were literally sown into their clothes for the winter.

My wife pointed out that all the teachers looked old even though they were only in their thirties.

Children were taught to have reverence for the dead and to stand still if they saw a funeral procession coming down the road. Of course funerals were generally more of a social event at that time. The whole street or, in a small village, the whole community would draw their curtains and wear black armbands to show respect for the dead.

Good table manners were taught by parents such as never talk with your mouth full, chew silently, empty your mouth before putting in more food. Grace would usually be said.

Children would have to change into play clothes when they came home from school. They were not allowed to play outside on Sundays but were often expected to go for a family walk. They were not allowed to sew or knit but could read or do jigsaws. My wife remembers that as they had candles in their bedroom they could play at making finger shadows in the flickering light on the wall.

Even in the days of horse-drawn transport the roads were dangerous. A favourite game with boys was getting a ride by hanging on the back of a cart. Boys often fell off and were injured. The drivers tried to discourage them by slashing their whips round the back of the cart.

Then and Now

I suppose that the main difference between childhood before the Second World War and today lies in the way in which children are treated by adults. In those days children were strictly disciplined in all classes of society, both at school and in the home. There was no hesitation in using corporal punishment and in my experience this was a definite deterrent. I never received the cane at school but seeing others caned deterred me from misbehaving. I believe it had the same effect on most children. In my school physical punishment was seldom used and on the whole the children were well behaved. Violence against a teacher was unthinkable for we were brought up to respect our teachers and indeed all adults. The mugging of old people was almost unknown though it is true that some children played tricks on the elderly, and made fun of anyone who was 'odd'. Such behaviour, however, was kept in check by parents, the local policeman or other adults who were not prevented by the law from punishing children they caught misbehaving.

Damage to property was also limited in this way for most adults felt they had a duty to society to protect their neighbours from crime. Many working-class people left their doors unlocked with no fear that they would be robbed.

Summary punishment by the constable or other adults seems to have been more effective in deterring offenders than the later system of children's courts.

Other attitudes have also changed. An important element in modern life today is excitement, and the pursuit thereof. We got our excitement in the country by climbing trees, scrumping apples, hunting rabbits, killing rats, following the 'Hunt', rather than in harming people, stealing cars and 'joyriding', or taking drugs, which are sadly the ways in which some of today's children satisfy their need for excitement. We had lower expectations and were easily satisfied. We did not expect to ride in cars. One of our highest ambitions was to own a bike. Harvest was an exciting time, so was threshing day and above all the annual fair that came to most country towns. Indeed, for most of the year we made our own amusements.

Most of my correspondents agree that their childhood was a happy time and look back perhaps with regret at this lost paradise, when families were close and the pleasures of life simple.

FURTHER READING

Aries, P.,   *Centuries of Childhood*, Penguin, Harmondsworth, 1973

Bloomfield, Marthena, *The Bulleymung Pit*, Faber, London, 1946
Nuts in the Rookery, Faber, London, 1946
Bow Net and Water Lilies, Faber, London, 1948

Burrows, R.,   *Beckery Burrows*, Research Publishing, London, 1978

Fay, J., and
  Martin, R.,   *The Jubilee Boy*, Filkins Press, Gloucestershire, 1987

Hillyer, R.,   *Country Boy*, Hodder and Stoughton, London, 1966

Horn, Pamela,   *The Victorian Country Child*, Roundwood Press, Kineton, 1974

Hutchinson, R.,   *Memories of a Village Childhood Over 60 Years Ago*, Best Print, Norton, Malton, Yorks., 1991

Jones, Llewelyn,   *Schoolin's Log*, Michael Joseph, London, 1980

Linnell, J.E.,   *Old Oak*, Burlington Press, Northampton, 1984

Nelson, G.K.,   *To Be A Farmer's Boy*, Alan Sutton, Stroud, 1991
                 Countrywomen on the Land, Alan Sutton, Stroud, 1992

Pinchbeck, I., and   *Children in English Society*, Routledge, London, 1973
  Hewett, M.,

Strange, Alf,   *Me Dad's the Village Blacksmith*, Gee, Denbigh, 1986

Strickland, I.,   *The Voices of Children 1700–1914*, Blackwell, Oxford, 1973

Uttley, A.,   *The Country Child*, Faber, London, 1931